My Father,
my Daughter

My Father, my Daughter

Pilgrims on the Road to Santiago

Donald Schell
and
Maria Schell

A
JourneyBook™
from
Church Publishing Incorporated New York

Library of Congress Cataloging-in-Publication Data

Schell, Donald.
    My father, my daughter : pilgrims on the road to Santiago / Donald
Schell and Maria Schell.
        p. cm.
    ISBN 0-89869-339-X (pbk.)
    1. Christian pilgrims and pilgrimages—Spain—Santiago de
Compostela. 2. Schell, Donald—Journeys—Spain, Northern. 3. Schell,
Maria—Journeys—Spain, Northern. 4. Spain, Northern—Description and
travel.   I. Schell, Maria. II. Title.
  BX2321.S3 S34 2001
  263'.0424611—dc21

                              2001017287

Cover photograph: Rick Strange/Index Stock

Church Publishing Incorporated
445 Fifth Avenue
New York, NY 10016
5 4 3 2 1

"Go and walk through the land and describe it." — *Joshua 18:8*

"It is solved by walking." —*Latin Proverb*

"Feet! Do your stuff!" —Lord John Whorfin, in *The Adventures of Buckaroo Banzai*

• • •

We offer this book with great love and thanks to our family, Ellen, Sasha & Arturo, Peter, Josh, and Rick; to writing companions Alan, Barbara, Belen, Buck, Catherine, Frank, Meleah, and Norma; to all who walked before us and with us; and those who are still on the path.

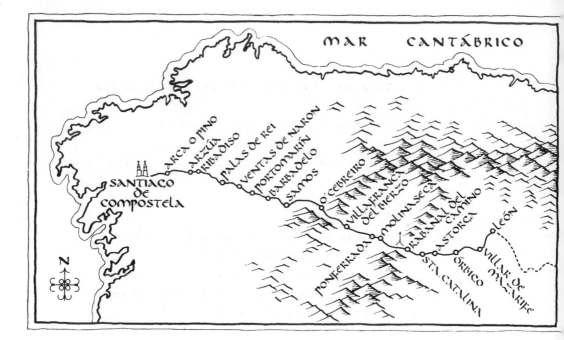

MAR CANTÁBRICO

SANTIAGO DE COMPOSTELA

ARCA O PINO
ARZÚA
RIBADISO
PALAS DE REI
VENTAS DE NARON
PORTOMARÍN
BARBADELO
SAMOS
O'CEBREIRO
VILLAFRANCA DEL BIERZO
MOLINASECA
PONFERRADA
RABANAL DEL CAMINO
ASTORGA
STA. CATALINA
ÓRBIGO
LEÓN
VILLAR DE MAZARIFE

N

MAR CANTÁBRICO

N

ST. JEAN
PIED-DE-PORT

RONCES-
VALLES

ZUBIRI

ARRE

PAMPLONA

PUENTE LA REINA

ESTELLA

VIANA

LOGROÑO

NÁJERA

ARCOS

STO. DOMINGO
DE LA CALZADA

BELORADO

S. JUAN DE ORTEGA

BURGOS

CASTROJERIZ

FROMISTA

CARRION DE
LOS CONDES

EL CAMINO
DE SANTIAGO

Map drawing by Pietro Calogero

IN JULY OF 1998 my younger daughter walked the pilgrimage to Santiago in Spain, and I went with her. This book will tell part of our story, an account of our walk. It is a progress report. More than we knew at the time, Maria and I walked because we both had work to do, some of it our own, some of it together. My work was to walk out of a depression.

By 1998 I had been working at St. Gregory's Episcopal Church for eighteen years. In a generation there, I had accomplished a great deal that I felt proud of. I had helped found a tiny group that grew into a thriving middle-sized congregation. I had overseen design and construction of a wonderful new church building. I had grown in my teaching and preaching. All things I had hoped I would do when I'd been ordained, but what lay ahead?

A mutual ministry review provoked half a dozen letters filled with anger and frustration at me and the other founding pastor. In these letters I didn't recognize us. I was wholly unprepared for such criticism. It hurt.

I was left brushing off suicidal thoughts like noisy, swarming mosquitoes. In the range of suicidal thinking it wasn't that bad. Nobody dies of mosquito bites. I had been far closer in 1973 when my first marriage was ending. But I scared myself one morning when I woke thinking, "If they want to kill the rector, maybe I should just do it for them." I stopped myself, "No, if that's how they feel, I should just move on." The calm logic in these thoughts felt dangerous.

I told Ellen, my wife, what I was thinking. She asked me to call the psychiatrist who had been so helpful to me some years before. I called and left a message. I felt better immediately.

A couple of days later he was telling me he would work with my depression, but that we'd get nowhere if I stuck with my exaggerated performance commitment and compulsions

. . . . . .

about work. He could deal with my spirit, but I needed to change the way I was working.

I was fifty-one and I'd lost my sense of direction. I wanted to believe there were good years ahead, but for the first time in my life, I had no idea what was next. Over the next couple of months, talking to the psychiatrist and people in the church helped. When Maria called home from college in New England with her plan to walk the pilgrimage, I responded without thinking, "Can I go with you?" **D**

Getting There
. . . . . .

MY OBSESSION WITH SPAIN began when I was fifteen and I went to live with a Spanish family for the summer. It was my first real trip without my parents. I was intrigued enough to return my junior year in college as a student at the University of Córdoba. It was then I embraced the Spanish pace, wandering the streets, dragging a slow day into night, gently wasting time in smoky bars and cafés.

That year, escape brought me to Spain. I ran from a failed love I had left in California. Since I was at college in Massachusetts, Justin and I were three thousand miles apart. Still, we were a knot, any attempts to pull us apart making our bond tighter.

We tried friendship for a while. He called me late one night and asked, "If we are friends, why can't I talk about Nina?" I then knew the width of the country was not enough distance between us. My talk of taking a year abroad became impassioned. In Spain, I thought, I would find someone easy to love and easy to leave. My Spaniard and I would speak quickly and fluidly in a language that Justin couldn't understand. Instead I went, spent ten wonderful months in Spain falling in love with the rugged Spanish landscape. I left knowing I would return.

I first learned of the pilgrimage from a tiny account I read in my student guidebook. Before graduation I had accepted an assistant teaching job back home that would start the following September. I was panicking at the thought of being so near Justin again when I got a letter from Paqui, my closest friend in Spain. Her boyfriend Raul's new job meant they could finally marry. It sounded wonderful. I could attend her wedding in July and spend the rest of my summer walking to Santiago.

I was willing to walk alone, but thoughts of Dad kept creeping in. It seemed logical, comforting even, to imagine the two of us walking together. But I didn't ask, scared he might say no. To my surprise when I called and told him of my plans, he invited himself along. And just like that we became partners, a seamless beginning.

After that first call, many others followed. He wanted more details and wanted me to help him find them. He treated our trip like a research project, searching for books to read, people to "interview." He wanted answers to his questions, which multiplied daily. What if it rains? What if we don't have enough food? What if they don't believe we are pilgrims? What if the water is bad and we get sick? What if we get lost? What if we get hurt? Will we need to bring a cell phone?

A cell phone? What kind of trip did Dad think this was? At college I was surrounded by seniors throwing themselves at the feet of business recruiters for the honor of a seventy-hour workweek. It was the world of cell phones and certainty, a world that I desperately wanted to escape. I decided to ignore Dad's requests for help. He wanted to know where we were going. I just wanted to get away. *M*

. . . . .

A Place to Begin
· · · · · ·

WHAT DID WE KNOW about the pilgrimage, really? Looking for practical information, we found a medieval history and journals of many modern pilgrims. Santiago de Compostela became a popular pilgrimage site after the miraculous "discovery" of Saint James's bones. According to legend, shortly after his death followers of Saint James brought his beheaded remains from Palestine to Spain for burial near what is now the city of Santiago. Eight hundred years passed before the burial site was rediscovered during the height of the Christian re-conquest of Spain. Christians, fighting hard against Muslims in the south, showed their might by building a huge Romanesque cathedral to replace the tiny church where Saint James was buried.

In the early years of the pilgrimage, enthusiastic monks embellished tales of God blessing Christian warriors. Visions in religious art showed a soldier Sant-Iago (Saint James) riding his horse in the sky over the battlefield, wielding his sword and beheading Moorish enemies. Medieval public relations invented the package—revelations of the identity of old bones; confirming visions; Saint James as *Matamoros,* the Moor Slayer; and pilgrimage—and Europe bought it whole.

Royal patrons built bridges and roads. Pious nobles donated beautiful churches and hospitals for pilgrims, and settlements grew around them. Soon a military road and promise of a heavenly reward drew a steady traffic of knights and armed retainers, all ready to follow the example of Matamoros. Ladies, gentlemen, monks, and nuns from all corners of Europe made vows to Saint James and walked the pilgrimage.

Saint Francis was one of these pilgrims, walking the Camino from Assisi on foot. The year he walked, he was one of a million or so along the route. More and more ordinary people, merchants, peasants, tradesmen, walked to fulfill a vow, looking for blessing and

· · · · · ·

healing. All over Europe people were buried with a scallop shell, the badge of their pilgrimage.

The pilgrimage never disappeared from modern history but waned until the European Union re-sparked interest. In 1998 seven thousand other pilgrims walked with us. The number continues to grow each year. Most modern pilgrims walk the *"Camino Frances"* as we did. Beginning at Saint Jean Pied de Port where many of the French portions of the Camino converge, this route crosses the Pyrenees to Roncesvalles where *refugios*, very cheap, simple hostels reserved for pilgrims, begin lining the Camino. *M*&**D**

O t i s
. . . . . .

OTIS, A FRIEND I'd known for quite a while, had walked the pilgrimage. We had never talked about it. I asked him to lunch so he could answer my questions, hoping he might also tell me what questions I had overlooked.

When I arrived to pick him up for lunch, Otis had laid out his pilgrim *credencias*, news and magazine clippings of pilgrim stories, postcards and pilgrim guides. He showed me his pilgrim's shell, staff and hat. I noted the title and publisher of the Spanish pilgrim's guide he recommended. This was progress. At lunch, some of my questions eluded me. I did ask what the path was like. I asked if there were always spaces in *refugios*. I asked about weather. Otis said he had walked in the spring and in the fall. He couldn't tell us about summer weather or about how crowded the *refugios* would be. I asked about sightseeing, since we'd be passing so many Romanesque churches. Otis said that the pilgrimage wasn't really like that. I decided he was less interested in architecture and history than I am.

He explained the letter I would need from the bishop.

. . . . . .

He talked of becoming friends with the people who walked or stayed together. Actually, he said, he had often walked alone but with friends and acquaintances in sight.

I asked about equipment. He told me to get good boots and break them in well before leaving. I said my hiking boots were well worn in and comfortable. Other things he said we would easily find in Spain. I pushed for a list of essentials, but his answer seemed unbelievably minimal: Good boots, walking shorts, T-shirt, a hat, staff, a light rain poncho, a sleep-sack, long pants, a change of underwear, second T-shirt, extra socks, and overshirt in case of cold, maybe a container for carrying water, and a good, small pack for carrying all this.

What about a tent, I asked?

"Some carry them," he said.

What about clothing appropriate to towns?

"No need."

Cooking equipment?

Plastic containers for carrying food?

"No need."

How much food should we carry?

"Not much."

Camera, books, journal, travelers checks?

"Travel light," he shrugged.

This was not my idea of a "Short List of Things to Do Before Beginning a Santiago Pilgrimage." Some of my questions seemed too small or foolish to ask. Did people walk in a clump or in a row? How did people dress and bathe in the co-ed *refugios*? Would Maria and I need to establish that we were father and daughter to room together in Spanish hotels?

I wanted to hear about an ordinary pilgrim day. "Start early," he said. I wanted to get beneath my simple questions to soul and spirit questions of inner preparation. I wanted to hear that Maria was right, and that we would be OK. I thought Otis was refusing to teach me. I couldn't see that what I wanted I would have to learn by walking. Otis was just offering himself as a fellow pilgrim.

After lunch I e-mailed Maria with the title of the guidebook. I told her I'd pay for the phone call if she'd order it from Spain. She thanked me for the note and said she was looking forward to graduation. With repeated requests and prodding, Maria finally said she was confident she would have time in Spain to get the book before I arrived.

But what if the booksellers tell us they could only get the book in a week? How would we solve that as we went along?

Another bookstore, she said. **D**

My Boots

. . . . .

THE BROWN SALOMON BOOTS were my first purchase for our walk. As I left the small outdoor equipment store in my college town I could feel my trip sliding out of the realm of talk and into the world of money. The boots were expensive; more money than I had ever spent on a single item of clothing, but their purchase verified what I had wanted for months. I would be a pilgrim. Even before I had my plane ticket I walked in my boots, trying to convince myself that I found them attractive. Held tight by a pair of spiral-patterned brown and red laces, they looked large and heavy on my feet. I saw the laces as a failed attempt to make function stylish.

I like shoes. I like hunting for the perfect pair, ones that blend fashion and comfort. But this time I couldn't afford to pay attention to my vanity, the stakes were too high. I chose them because they were the most comfortable pair I could find. I heard of people taking

. . . . .

two pairs of boots, which I had decided not to do. I couldn't afford to pick the wrong pair.

When I first arrived at the store, I threw myself at the mercy of a fifteen-year-old sales "man," who directed me to a pair of wool socks. "Every good boot starts with a good pair of socks," he declared as he threw a pair of gray hiking-weight "smartwools" to me. "These will do everything you'll need." Like finish the term paper I should be writing, I silently retorted.

With my new socks on, he showed me several pairs of boots, some low, some high, some leather and some not. Finally he brought out the Salomons. "These," he said slightly under his breath, "these, are *really* good boots." A woman hiker who overheard our conversation readily agreed. They had "Gore-Tex lining," "removable dual cushion insoles," and the treads said "Contragrip" in flashy red letters. I wasn't sure what these extras did, but I noticed the other boots didn't have them. A good sign, I decided.

I took my boots home, and tended to them like newborn twins. I showed them off to my friends and covered them in creams and treatments to make them soft and supple. I went walking with them every morning.

The wool socks felt marvelous but the stiff and unforgiving boots hurt. When not on my feet I stretched them, twisting and bending them vengefully. With only two months until we left, I wore them everywhere. I had to break them in or they would give me blisters. This made me hate them all the more. *M*

· · · · · ·

Credencias
· · · · · ·

June 18, 1998
To the Keepers of the Pilgrims' Way
And hosts at Pilgrim Refuges

Greetings in the name of God.

The bearer of this letter, Father Donald Schell, a priest of the Diocese of California in the Protestant Episcopal Church in the United States of America, and Maria Schell, his daughter, are traveling to Spain with my blessing to walk as pilgrims on the Camino to Santiago de Compostela.

I know them and can attest that they will walk the Camino devoutly, remembering in gratitude the countless pilgrims who have preceded them. Both Donald and Maria bring with them their love of Spain, their interest in Christian history, and their appreciation of the Spanish people. They are Christians of good faith and character, trustworthy guests for any pilgrim's refuge and good companions to any pilgrims who may walk with them.

Please extend to them the welcome, hospitality, and acknowledgment given to true pilgrims.

Given by my hand and seal,
The Rt. Rev. William E. Swing
Bishop of California

I wrote this letter myself for the bishop to sign.

The guidebooks said we needed an ecclesiastical letter of introduction to get our *credencias* (credentials to stay in cheap or free pilgrim *refugios*). Our books said a letter from a parish priest was adequate, but I decided a letter from the bishop, although it would make clear

· · · · · ·

that we were Episcopalians, might still impress the Spanish Roman Catholic monk I imagined would review our letter.

I phoned the bishop. His secretary returned my call and said he would happily sign our letter after she had re-typed it on his stationery.

I crafted his letter with great care, thinking of Sir Walter Raleigh writing of pilgrim shells and staffs in days when Anglicans couldn't go to Spain. Ellen (my wife) and Rick (co-founder of Saint Gregory's) both thought my letter solemn enough to be used as a reference for the Boy Scouts' God and Country Award. I agreed that it did sound a little formal, but I didn't want to risk something that "wouldn't work," though I wasn't sure what "wouldn't work" might mean.

Convinced Maria would never get to it, I e-mailed the letter to her older sister, Sasha, in England to translate into Spanish. I wanted two signed copies, one in Spanish, one in English. Both copies would bear the bishop's signature, making each an original, which I appreciated.

I liked imagining the Spanish monk reading Bishop Swing's signature above his title, "Obispo de California." But would it concern the monk that the bishop's seal was not on the letter? The Spanish was clear on this point, "Dado por mi mano y *sello.*" But it would have to do. I had other preparations to worry about.

When I got them back, I carried both letters, English and Spanish, with me every day. I liked to read them aloud. Hearing the Spanish, I felt we really would be pilgrims. I imagined our excitement at showing the letters to the monk at Roncesvalles who would give us our *credencias.* In *refugios* all across Spain we would watch *hospitaleros* stamp these *credencias* with distinctive *sellos*, just like I'd seen on the *credencias* of returned pilgrims. **D**

. . . . . .

The Wedding
· · · · · ·

AFTER THE LONG PLANE RIDE to Madrid I took the first train south to Córdoba. I came looking for old friends and found them all gone. The few acquaintances left in the city treated my presence as little more than an oddity. Still days before the wedding, I phoned Paqui in her hometown, Fuente Tojar, some two hours from the city. She invited me to her house, but I did not want to be a burden during her final days of preparation. She was too tired to insist. The invitation was lost.

She told me she had arranged for me to travel to her town with her college friends, none of whom I knew. I would wait in Córdoba until then. Finding myself with nothing to do, I wandered familiar streets like a tourist. Buildings I loved felt empty. Seeing them left a dry taste in my mouth, like yellow cake with no frosting.

The day of the wedding I waited at the appointed corner, my dress and wedding present in tow. I felt like a package waiting for delivery. I scanned the crowd wondering which one might be Ana. Someone called out my name. The voice belonged to an attractive girl, a friendly face, though unfamiliar. Ana introduced me to everyone in our two-car caravan. After a bit of discussion about how best to divide the group, I rode with Ana, her boyfriend, José, and Monica. Ana insisted I take the front seat, honoring the distance I had traveled to get to the wedding. She told me how pleased Paqui was I had come. Monica traded gossip about her favorite Spanish singers for my bits of information about California. Time passed quickly.

Paqui had warned me on my first visit that Fuente Tojar was not one of the picturesque "white towns" featured in guidebooks. Instead of charming white buildings providing a pristine canvas for hundreds of wall-mounted flower pots, Fuente Tojar's white walls stood

· · · · · ·

starkly bare. At 6 p.m. in the harsh sunlight, I thought of Paqui's words. But I hadn't come for the scenery.

As friends of the bride, we were supposed to escort Paqui in the traditional walk from her house to the church. I worried we were arriving too late for this ritual. But as if on cue, just as we parked the car in front of her house, Paqui stepped out into the street. A crowd gathered around her. We joined them.

The late afternoon sun shining on her melted her white dress, light on light, into the radiant white walls of the town. With her long train and transparent veil flowing behind her she seemed not to walk at all, but float downhill toward the church. I held my breath in awe. She waved at me and smiled. I was filled with pride. In that moment, it didn't matter that the streets of the town were concrete and not cobblestone. Fuente Tojar had found its adornment.

The church, too small to hold everyone, overflowed with guests. No one minded. Children played in the garden outside the church. I stood quietly at the back, entranced by the traditional Romeria music sung to honor the bride and groom. At the reception, people I had met only briefly welcomed me as family. Generosity flowed like wine. With the sweet taste of wedding cake in my mouth, everything seemed possible. *M*

Have Stick, Will Travel

· · · · · ·

WHEN I GRADUATED FROM SEMINARY in 1971, new to the Episcopal Church, I had only a tentative job offer for the fall. Sasha was eighteen months old. Her mother and I were traveling with her in Britain, struggling to make sense of our future, when I got a call telling me the job offer had fallen through. We had nothing to go back to.

· · · · · ·

Late that summer, staring West from the coast of Wales, I watched a low sun halo Bardsey Island's dark cliffs in radiant gold. I longed to walk that island as pilgrims had since the sixth century, but it was a closed bird refuge. Images of that island haunted me through the pain of divorce, and the joy of life with Ellen.

Twenty-five years later, I held Ellen's hand and stared again at Bardsey, a dark mountain rising from the sea. We had taken the children to Britain to visit Sasha in graduate school. That evening Ellen asked at the bed and breakfast about Bardsey and learned that now, anyone willing to brave an hour-long speed boat ride on the rough chop of the Irish Sea could visit it. We called the charter boat.

Early next morning we walked down a narrow path to the tiny inlet where our boat waited. Outside the inlet, the waves pounded against the boat relentlessly as the wind howled. For medieval pilgrims, this last part of the journey, ferried out by oarsmen hauling against wind and waves, was the toughest part. Many were lost on the way.

No one spoke during the long ride. The boatman let us ashore in the island's only sheltered cove.

The far side of the island was covered in yellow fields of mustard. We walked up the stony mountain to Saint Mary's well, where I picked up a pebble as medieval pilgrims had. I planned to bury it in the foundation of the church we were building in San Francisco.

Hiking back to meet the boat that afternoon, we passed the gift shop, open and untended, a cash bowl signed simply, "payment as marked." Walking sticks in an umbrella stand reminded me of ancient pilgrims. I had no practical use for a walking stick, but I tried several and bought a shoulder-high reddish one, for its polished gnarls where tiny branches once sprouted. Back home I leaned it in the corner of the bedroom where it stayed for two years.

When I invited myself on Maria's pilgrimage, I thought of the stick. I hoped to befriend the stick and feel its purpose. I practiced walking with it on the hills of San Francisco, ignoring the people that stared at me. The end of the stick started to wear a little, so I bought a hard rubber foot to protect it from splintering. I bought a second foot for Maria's stick. **D**

The Gun
. . . . .

AFTER THE WEDDING I returned alone to Córdoba. Paqui had left on her honeymoon and I wondered why I had planned so much extra time in the city. I found myself drifting through the streets, desperate for some distraction. I passed the Mezquita, a huge eighth-century mosque that sat majestically in the center of the old city. Standing in its patio, I watched busloads of tourists descending on the massive building. I wanted to sit quietly and think, but there were too many people; I decided to return in the afternoon. I headed to the Zoco, a traditional marketplace where artisans made and sold their work.

As I walked through the Zoco, a silver shell bracelet in a shop display caught my eye. "Pilgrim Shell!" I thought. Jewelry seemed impractical and vain on a pilgrimage, but I was tempted and bored. I entered the tiny shop. The entire room was no more than a few feet wide, almost every inch of it covered with tools, boxes, pins, and unfinished jewelry. Only the display case indicated it was a business. I liked it. It was alive with work and all the mess that work produces.

A man, a little older than my father, sat at a workbench, fussing at a pair of earrings. "*Sientate, Guapa*," he called to me, smiling and pointing to a chair. He seemed a nice man. I sat down right by the door, barely inside the shop. I asked about his work. He smiled,

. . . . . .

pleased to hear I had done some jewelry making in high school. I told him about my pilgrimage. He showed me one of the shell bracelets and told me he had made seven hundred more but had yet to make the trip north to Santiago to sell them.

It was a relief to have someone to talk to. His name was Javier, and he was a native of the city. We talked about the United States, a country he admired very much. He preferred the brash youth of America to Spain's tired history. "Here, we worship what is dead. The Mezquita is nice but it is old. Why not tear it down and build something new and even better?" he mused.

He wanted to know where I was staying and if I was alone. Slightly uncomfortable with his questions I lied, letting him believe I was staying at a friend's house. Perhaps I'd misunderstood. It had been a while since I had spoken Spanish. He poured two glasses of sherry. I decided not to accept this drink unless he drank as well, and only if I could choose my own glass. As I sipped on the thick sweet liquid, Javier began to ask me more personal questions, touching my bare leg as he asked them.

I tried to steer the conversation back to Spain. What a wonderful place where you never have to worry about someone pulling a gun on you, I pointed out. "Oh no," he said. "Don't be fooled by our gun laws. Spaniards have guns." He offered to show me his.

Then he offered to let me stay at his house.

Then he offered to let me stay in his bed.

I am alone. I want to leave but he might follow me.

In his hand he held my already-paid-for bracelet. If I leave without it, he will think something is wrong. I only got the bracelet by promising to return so he could make me a matching pendent. I left with the bracelet in hand. Now it sits in the bottom of my jewelry box. I have yet to wear it. *M*

· · · · ·

Being Alone
. . . . .

I RETURNED TO MY HOSTEL tired and hungry. I felt dumb for not seeing Javier as the dirty old man he was. Wanting to forget as much of the day as possible, I decided to get an early dinner and head to bed. I set out for Picantón, a favorite sandwich counter from my year as a student. It was early still, and the tiny place was abandoned as I ordered my dinner. "This is my Córdoba," I thought as the familiar old man slathered my crunchy white roll with "red" and "green" sauce, obscuring the lettuce, tomato and grilled chicken. I happily took my warm sandwich in its white paper, and headed out to the street.

With the tourists gone I went back to the courtyard of the Mezquita. I sat in the shade watching the warm wind rustling the leaves of the orange trees. It was easy to imagine Muslim pilgrims crowding the fountain to wash feet, hands and heads before entering the Mezquita for prayer.

I began my dinner, unwrapping the sandwich from its white paper. I stretched my watering mouth around the sandwich, longing for the familiar taste. Green sauce dripped down my hands and arms. But before I could bite down, pain seized me. The gums behind my molars were so sore and swollen that the toasted bread scraped my mouth like sandpaper.

I had been having trouble with my gums before I left for Spain, and went so far as to call my mother for her opinion as a nurse. She said not to worry, they were probably just irritated and would heal in a couple of days. If they still bothered me I could go to the dentist when I got back home.

This was fine advice when I could still eat, but now what? I tried to force chewing. This aggravated my gums more. I re-wrapped the remaining portion of the sandwich in its white paper and placed it next to the trash.

Panic set in. I had no idea how to find a dentist in Córdoba. Medical attention on the

. . . . .

Camino might be hard to come by. The following day I would leave for Barcelona to met Dad. I didn't know the Spanish word for gums.

I went back to my hotel determined to forget the problem. I paced my small room like a caged animal. I searched through the contents of my backpack, knowing I would find nothing for gums. Through my small window I watched the sun disappear behind the Mezquita, leaving me completely alone.

Rest would calm me, I was certain, but fear kept me alert and awake. The restaurant below my window was noisy with tourists enjoying dinner. Their happy clanging of dishes made me angry. I wanted to shut the noise out, but it was too warm to close the window. I lay on my bed wishing I would cry.

I don't remember drifting off that night. I only remember waking the next morning, relieved I had slept at least a little. My gums still sore, I managed a soft croissant and some orange juice for breakfast. After some last-minute errands, it was time to take the overnight train to Barcelona to meet Dad.

On the train, I shared my compartment with a pair of sisters going away for the summer. The younger sister, no more than eleven, cried. Her first trip without parents. I offered her my upper bunk for the better view. In return, she offered me crackers and cheese. I accepted them gladly, munching on them as we chatted about America. Only now do I realize that I did this without pain. I drifted off with the rocking of the train and awoke rested and eager to met Dad. *M*

"IF YOU are continuing on to ...."

To Spain, I thought. We were over Scotland, and the stewardess was distributing landing cards for Britain. As she finished, I called her to explain I was only stopping for breakfast in Heathrow with my daughter. "Lovely," she said.

Yes, but would I need a landing card?

"Hardly seems so. Won't your daughter simply meet you at the gate?"

At the gate? Sasha had my flight information, but we hadn't agreed where to meet. I was arriving at one crowded terminal and leaving from another. We could easily spend two and a half hours looking for each other. I was carrying a thousand dollars cash from her San Francisco savings account. If we didn't connect, she'd be without the cash she needed, and I'd be stuck carrying it across Spain. Where would she look for me?

"Damn," I muttered, glancing at my watch. In ten minutes of failing to figure this out we had flown a hundred miles closer to Heathrow. Time was running out.

Where would she look for me? Think like Sasha! If she were the one flying in, she would have sent me to her departure gate so we could stay in one place. If I hoofed it to my departing terminal, she'd probably be there waiting. I filled out the landing card. On the line asking purpose of my visit to Britain I wrote, "Breakfast with my daughter," an eccentric but pleasing answer. "Cash delivery" would raise too many questions.

The moment the plane stopped, I stood, dragged my pack from the overhead bin, hoisted it to my shoulders, clasped my walking stick, crowned myself with my straw pilgrim's hat, and rushed out with the crowd. British immigration barely glanced at my landing card. With the river of arriving passengers I was swept round the corner and into a sea of faces, all look-

. . . . . .

ing for someone. I didn't see her. What if she didn't find me here and went looking at the other terminal?

Fresh faces kept appearing at the escalator. I guessed she would come this way and I stood like a rock in the way. With my walking stick planted in front of me I could study each face as it came into view. People parted around me.

Sasha appeared, staring at me with no sign of recognition. "Sasha!" I said. "Dad?" she laughed, stepping off the escalator to hug me. She pulled us from the flood of people, stepped back to look, and explained that my threatening-looking stick, red beard with white chin hairs, and outlandish straw hat had her wondering whether this strange-looking man thought he was some kind of prophet.

She treated me to a sumptuous East Indian breakfast. I handed off her thousand dollars under the table. She said she was impatient to finish graduate work and wished she could walk the pilgrimage with us. I asked about her love life. "Nonexistent," she said, "and please don't ask about Arturo." Reminding me that she was the one who had walked to Machu Pichu, she expressed her concern that Maria was an unlikely walker and asked about the rest of the family.

It was time to board for Barcelona. Sasha asked me to give Maria greetings, love and best wishes. I wished her productive writing.

White fog covering the channel gave way to the homely patchwork of French farms. We flew southeast toward the Pyrenees, which rose as a stony wall before us. Could Maria and I handle these mountains?

The sun flashed silver on deep blue water as we landed by a palm-lined beach. Tightly packed houses and buildings radiated warm, gold light. They stretched across the level building space and flowed up rugged, sandy-gold mountains. "Pilgrim?" I thought, "Barcelona looks just like California."

. . . . . .

Maria shouted "*Hola*, Daddy!" pulling me from the crowd for a hug. She studied my boots and showed me hers, ruffled my new beard, and admired my hat and walking stick's rubber tip. "Now Dad, I'm going to show you one of my favorite cities." **D**

Taking Inventory

· · · · ·

MY TRAIN ARRIVED IN BARCELONA mid-morning, giving me enough time to check into the hotel and head out to meet Dad's plane. In the airport my walking stick felt awkward on the smooth polished concrete, and even more so on the escalator. I didn't blame the business travelers and tourists who stared. I didn't belong and I knew it. I felt relieved and excited to see Dad as he emerged with the other passengers, a familiar grin shining through his wildman red beard. With our walking sticks and hats we were a pair, equally misplaced in the airport.

I had plans for the day, but Dad thought it important to unpack and take inventory first. Once en route it would be days before we passed through a major city. This was our chance to get any overlooked supplies. We headed to the hotel.

After showering and settling into our room, we compared walking sticks. Dad had brought his from Bardsey, a medieval pilgrims' isle off Wales. Mine was from a strip mall in New Jersey. I didn't tell Dad I had bought the walking stick for his benefit. To me walking sticks were the toys of bored child hikers and theatrical outdoorsmen who envisioned themselves as Moses. But Dad was certain sticks would prove useful, so I got one.

We turned our attention to our packs. Mine, a more standard backpacking bag, had a long sack with an internal frame and a few side pockets. Dad's, also with an internal frame, looked more like an oversized school pack. "The saleswoman assured me this was the bet-

· · · · ·

ter kind for our trip," he said. "I can get at anything I need without totally unpacking," he demonstrated, opening and closing the side pockets. True, but my pack was large enough to use for longer, more serious backpacking trips.

We compared each other's bags for weight. I had gotten my pack down to a bare minimum, eighteen pounds. My sister Sasha, the avid traveler in our family, had taught me well. Packing for our trip I got rid of everything I could, going so far as to measure out lengths of dental floss so I wouldn't have to carry the dispenser. Dad thought this excessive. I smirked when he admitted his pack weighed twenty-three pounds.

He had a lot more stuff than I did, most of it religious. He carried with him a reduced bible he had made for the trip and a book on theology. He showed me the photos (an icon of Peter and Paul, and one of his seminary) he had taped to the inside cover of his journal. I wondered what kind of person I was traveling with. Most of his extra weight came from clothes. Seeing him unpack all those shirts, each carefully chosen for every weather eventuality, made me nervous. Had I counted too much on the heat?

Dad gave me the summer sleeping bag he had promised to bring me. It matched his own. Showing them to me he recounted his discussion with the saleswoman. He pointed out all the features that convinced him these were the right bags for our trip.

I presented him with a tiny flashlight, Dr. Bronner's all-purpose soap, a compass, and a small container of instant sanitizer. I explained the logic and significance of everything in my bag. I knew Dad could trust in a pilgrim companion who had the sense to bring safety pins. *M*

. . . . .

"WE'RE GOING TO WALK ALL DAY," Maria announced as I got off the plane, reminding me it was Sasha's proven therapy for jet lag—stay awake, walk until dark, mostly outdoors. On the metro downtown, she described what she'd accomplished that morning: purchasing train tickets for our overnight train to Hendaye, finding us a hotel and leaving off her backpack, and scouting a bookstore for our pilgrim guide, all after arriving on the night train from Córdoba. I was impressed.

From the metro stop downtown, she led us decisively upstairs through crowded markets, streets and alleys to our hotel.

"It's laundry time," Maria announced. She set to her hand-washing with a tiny bottle of space-saving condensed soap. I changed, and imitated her, washing my laundry, wringing things out and hanging them to dry.

"Okay," I said, "let's walk 'til we drop."

"Don't forget sun-block, Dad. We can't afford to burn."

The streets were full of people. We walked to the bookstore where we chose the Spanish original of the pilgrim's guide over an English translation. Then Maria led us to the Picasso Museum. A line of waiting people stretched round the block.

"We'll eat now," Maria directed. "After lunch there will be no line."

The restaurant she knew was closed. We walked past a safe, fancier café to a shabby-looking hole in the wall. "Do you know this place, Maria?" I asked.

"No, but it will be good, Dad. Trust me."

The food was excellent and cheap. The line for the museum was gone when we finished, and we devoured the Picassos as eagerly as we had lunch. We strode on to Gaudí's Sagrada

Familia Church. "When I was here before," Maria said, "I wanted to talk about its architecture with you. Now you're here."

We climbed all the towers, sharing startling perspectives on the building and the city, and didn't leave until closing. She led me to Las Ramblas, a busy shopping boulevard where she knew a tiny pita-and-kebab place. Delicious again. After dinner she guided us through twisting streets and alleys to the tony Four Cats Café. "It used to be really Bohemian," Maria explained, "when Picasso hung out here as a young painter. For our budget, it's just beers and dessert."

We went back to the hotel twenty-six hours after I'd gotten up in San Francisco. We had walked such a distance and climbed so many stairs that I slept easily and deeply. Next morning, Maria had us check out early, storing our packs at the hotel. We walked to Gaudí's Palacio Guell and wandered through, talking architecture again before the Palacio got crowded. As we hiked to the museum of Romanesque art on the hillside above the city, the heat felt good, though my feet hurt some. Final preparation for our pilgrimage, I thought.

We climbed a grand outdoor stairs to the museum. We lingered, wandering back to frescoes we'd particularly enjoyed, smiling beatifically at visitors who were just passing through. "I knew you'd love it," she said.

The sun was low. We walked back to our hotel to pick up packs, hats, and staffs. On the metro to the train station, dressed and equipped for hiking, our packs bumped commuters as the car swayed. We pulled in, holding our staffs close.

"*Peregrinos?*" a young woman asked.

"*Sí,*" Maria answered.

The woman spoke briefly of her own pilgrimage with a radiant smile and wished us *Buen Camino.* **D**

. . . . .

WE ATE OUR LAST DINNER in Barcelona in the train station. It was dark outside when the P.A. system called us to board. Walking down the endless platform we passed car after car before finding our own. We had a sleeper with a single narrow hallway, which opened on to a half dozen compartments. Our compartment was tight, three bunks high, two on each side, six bunks in all. We had the two highest.

There was no room for us to stand, so Dad and I climbed into our bunks. A luggage shelf ran over the door. I pushed hard on my pack to make sure it would not fall on me as I slept. The train crept out of the station and gathered speed. Sitting Indian-style with my back hunched against the wall, I felt how much the high bunks pitched and swayed as they echoed the rocking of the train. Being so high we collected all the heat of the small compartment. "This is miserable," I thought. I looked to my father for sympathy. Lying on his back, hands behind his head, he was the happy hobo, completely unvexed. I abandoned my bunk.

In the narrow hallway outside our compartment, I eavesdropped on the conversations of my train mates. Mostly they were college students in search of an "experience," blaring through country after country, bragging of their travel promiscuity. Leaning back against the cool window, I spoke to a group from New York. They were heading to Pamplona for the two-week long festival of San Fermín, the running of the bulls. I loathed their stories of grabbing, greedy sightseeing. Still, I wanted them to like me.

They asked questions about the pilgrimage, showing a sort of gawking interest in my trip. It sounded unglamorous and religious. And I was traveling with my father. They looked at me as if it was all too strange to be real. I wondered if they were right. Feeling old, I gave

. . . . . .

up on the conversation. They were college students, immersed in a world that I was no longer part of.

I climbed up into my bunk. The buzzing fan pushed warm, stale air in circles around me. Each breath left me tired and heavy. My eyes, unwilling to accept exhaustion, remained open as I lay silently on my back. I listened to Dad's snoring, his breath mimicking the hypnotic rhythm of the train. How had I gotten myself into this mess?

Hours passed. The compartment, lit only by the night-lights, was just bright enough to count the holes in the ceiling tiles. Insomnia would be easier in the dark, I thought to myself.

The train jolted to a stop. The sudden movement jerked Dad to his side producing one loud snort and then quiet breathing. In an instant the fan stopped and the lights went out. Silence. The monotony of sound in the cabin broke with a sequence of far-off low booms. I climbed out of bed and went into the hallway. Passengers filled the narrow space, quietly staring out the window. My bare feet felt good on the cold floor.

I squinted. In the darkness I saw only the distant silhouette of a church tower and a few lights around it. Suddenly green and yellow fireworks exploded, making a whole town momentarily visible. With each flash I could now see that the glimmering lights were but the reflection of the town in still water below. Was it the sea? Too confused to make sense of it, I watched the light bleed into its reflection. *M*

Lost

· · · · · ·

IT WAS 11:30 A.M. when we finally ended our train travels. I felt awful. My backpack seemed unbearably heavy. The cheese-and-egg baguette sandwich I'd eaten for breakfast wouldn't sit still in my stomach. I wanted a shower and long nap, but more than that I wanted to get on the road. From the train we walked into town. Saint Jean Pied de Port was quaint, its streets full of storybook houses accented by painted shutters, window boxes and perfectly maintained gardens. A living postcard of village France. If I hadn't been so worried about the road ahead, I might have wondered if Saint Jean really existed.

Dad thought that we should use up our bit of French money to buy food for the road. We found a small bakery and bought bread, dried figs and nuts. Our map showed the pilgrims' path beginning on the other side of town. To get there, we had to cross the open-air medieval marketplace, which in modern times had become a pilgrim strip mall, selling staffs, water gourds and shells. All of it captivated my father. He was like a child, seeing, pointing, going and touching, but always speaking with adult authority.

I was frustrated. It was noon and we hadn't gotten anywhere yet. Our guidebook warned of the long uphill first day. I knew Dad was strong. I would have to work hard to keep up. His detours seemed grossly unfair. I rolled my eyes with each suggestion.

Our guidebook gave two possible routes to Roncesvalles, one hard and the other harder. The first and more traditional, Napoleon's route, went directly up over the mountain on a small footpath. We read of people getting stuck on the steep wilderness path. Unable to finish before dark, they slept on the trail. The other, slightly shorter route climbed less dramatically, going by way of the old Roman road, which was now a highway. On the train Dad had said he wanted to walk Napoleon's route. I pointed out that we had no camping equipment and were starting late in the day. The shorter route was clearly our best choice.

· · · · · ·

Dad relented, but said he really wanted to cross the medieval pilgrim's bridge instead of the modern bridge that our guidebook dictated. His detour took us off our rough street map. Across the bridge we found ourselves in a residential area. A large metal pilgrim's sign pointed us up a hill away from the town.

Something was wrong. Our guidebook warned the shorter route ran next to a highway with heavy traffic, but we walked without a car in sight. It was steep toe walking, my heels never touching the ground. With each step I thought, I can't do this. I had encountered the impossible and impassable. The distance between Dad and me grew, as I struggled to keep up with his pace. I won't make it. I can't tell Dad. *M*

Wrong Road

· · · · · ·

SO, I STEERED US to the wrong road. Shortly after my medieval bridge, we saw a "Camino de Santiago" sign and followed it up into the hills. It was very steep. In a kilometer Maria was feeling quite discouraged, fearing failure in a way that I would only experience later. It got steeper. This was hard work for me, but Maria was panting and said her muscles were burning. We hadn't learned yet about warming up to the walk and finding our rhythm. We strained on. Fewer and fewer cars passed us. I mused aloud that we might be headed toward the higher pass. We kept walking.

This road seemed too quiet, but turning back is harder on foot than by car. Progress by car is time and gas. Walking costs energy and determination. Could we afford to admit we were lost and give up what we'd climbed? We walked the steep lane for another kilometer and then stopped.

· · · · · ·

Turning back also meant we didn't know where we were going. Back where I'd first thought we might be heading the wrong way, we found an old man pruning his roses. He was vague at reading maps and vague with directions, but his patience with my French inspired me. Roncesvalles, he insisted, was the direction we'd been heading, though he supposed a highway might well be back the way we had come. We headed back hoping to find someone who could read our map.

How could we have missed a highway? Would asking directions take us all the way back into the center of Saint Jean? I steered us down a road toward where I hoped we'd find our way. Maria no longer trusted my hunches in a countryside I knew not at all.

"We need to find someone and you need to ask directions," she said with quiet vehemence. We continued back toward town, seeing no one. I feared we'd have to retrace our steps back up this hill and over the high pass, but didn't say so.

We saw a mother and daughter getting in their car. "Ask them!" Maria said. I knew we depended here on my French, but I was shy and reluctant from my frustrating conversation with the old man.

"I can't do this myself," Maria insisted.

I asked, and the mother knew of the two routes to Roncesvalles. She pointed us down another residential street well short of town that would lead to the highway. They wished us luck and we continued. It was almost one o'clock. **D**

· · · · ·

AT OUR FIRST HIGHWAY SIGN we glanced at our map. Valcarlos was signed. Maria found it on the map. But where was the river? I pointed to the dense line of trees we saw beyond the fields. "Over there. Enough map," I said.

"Yes, let's walk."

Neither of us noticed that the map showed a footpath running up the valley on the shady side of those trees. The highway had no shoulder, so we began to walk briskly facing the traffic. Maria stayed on the pavement.

I tried walking the fence-mound between road and field. There was little room alongside the barbed-wire, and the tall, thick grass slowed my motion. I gave up and rejoined Maria. We watched ahead for oncoming trucks. When there was traffic on the other side, a truck had to reclaim the roadway from us. We'd step off to the fence-mound.

We watched hay-baling tractors gathering golden dry hay and spewing it out in man-high shredded-wheat shaped bales. The hay's mild, sweet caramel scent hung in the air. We marched on. I assured Maria we were doing all right.

At the mouth of a stony canyon the road and river converged. We left the open fields and followed the road up the canyon. The air hung still. Sun bore down on us and beat on bright rocky cliffs that reflected heat back. Sometimes I'd smell airport-like whiffs of exhaust, unburnt fuel and hot rubber. The occasional breaths of spray off the river exhilarated and relieved me. The highway twisted on. I welcomed the smallest turn of the road for its few moments of shade.

Again and again we heard the screech and squeal of truck brakes, an engine's growl and the squish of tires rushing down on hot pavement. At the first sound I'd look for a hollow in the cliff. I'd tell Maria to hold on to her hat, and we'd push toward safety, every muscle

· · · · · ·

poised to pull back from the air turbulence that would suck us toward the passing truck. Abruptly after it passed, hot wind would toss us the other way, back toward the cliff. Each time we'd quickly catch our balance and resume walking.

Sports cars, hurtling down without the punctuation of brake noise, pounced on us suddenly as a cat lunging toward a bird. We'd do our best to jump aside.

When drivers saw us in comfortable time, they often smiled and waved, sometimes offering a friendly honk, our first welcome as pilgrims. White wooden crosses low in the cliff face wouldn't let me forget the danger. Maria began to ask when we could take a break.

"Let's keep on until we find a safer place to stop," I said, using an old Dad trick. Whether she noticed my manipulation or not, she trudged on, complaining only slightly.

The road crossed a bridge and continued its climb up the other, mostly unshaded, side of the ravine. In a rare patch of shade at a hairpin turn we paused to drink deeply from our water bottles, savor our oranges and wonder where we'd find shade again.

Maria spotted Arneguy. We began to feel some progress as each twist of the road brought us closer to the village. We were both hot and tired. I hoped it would be a place to stop for lunch. **D**

A Rest

· · · · ·

WE APPROACHED ARNEGUY, one of two towns between us and Roncesvalles, where we would cross the border back into Spain. The road split. A sign directed all traffic down to a small border check and a restaurant-less, grocer-less town. The highway continued straight ahead. At the fork, one hundred meters away from the shed marked *"Policia,"* we stopped. It

· · · · ·

looked abandoned. "Let's skip this, Dad," I said. In all the times that I had traveled between France and Spain I never once had my passport stamped. He was skeptical. "If we go down there we will just have to climb back up," I said. This convinced him. We pressed on.

Two kilometers later we arrived at Valcarlos. Much larger than its neighbor, Valcarlos ran four blocks along the road. It boasted a hotel, a grocery store, and a newsstand. We stumbled into the hotel. I asked about lunch, hoping they would serve us in the bar. The restaurant seemed too nice a place for a pair of sweaty pilgrims still burdened with packs.

To my surprise the bartender called the hostess who graciously showed us to a white linen-covered table in a white-walled dining room. With exposed wooden ceiling beams and decorative pottery, the room might as well have been a Condé Nast's rustic dining layout. Dirty, tired and hardly able to speak, we didn't belong there. I didn't care. Neither, oddly enough, did our waitress.

Our table, meticulously set, had on it a small basket of bread and a clay pitcher of cold water. Both were empty before the waitress returned with menus. "You're thirsty," she noted, half asking half observing. "Yes." "I will bring more water," she said. "Thanks," I just managed to reply.

The waitress recited the menu of the day, the lunch deal available at almost every restaurant in Spain. It was about twice as expensive as I had planned for meals during our trip. I was expecting the pilgrimage to be cheap, cheap, cheap, but this was the only restaurant on our day's walk. I said nothing.

We ordered. Soup started the meal, "*Muy tipico*" she told us, the traditional fare of the region. It was hot and despite the heat of the day, this was good. Heat distinguished the hotel food from the cold food we carried in our packs. The meal kept coming. Even with three courses and dessert we had no trouble cleaning our plates. As we finished our dessert, all pain and the mountain ahead disappeared. I was just having lunch with my Dad. *M*

"LOOK, we leave the road!" Maria exclaimed, pointing to a highway sign marked "Camino de Santiago."

"Camino de Santiago?" I muttered, looking down a path carpeted with wildflowers. "No one has walked this way since spring." But Maria ran ahead and found the first of the small obelisks that we had read about, the ones that would mark the Camino. It was cast concrete, not quite hip-high and inset with a yellow tile scallop shell. An arrow below the tile pointed down the grassy path. We took photos of each other by the obelisk and left the road behind.

Quickly I found a painted yellow arrow, the more common Camino marker, according to the guidebook. More yellow arrows and the occasional concrete obelisk pointed us down toward the river. We heard it before we saw it, a cheerful mountain stream a dozen meters down a steep ravine. A missing bridge ended the path. Across the ravine, a vine-covered stone barn and farmhouse glistened green in hard sunlight. Torrents of a hundred winters had washed away any trace of the bridge. A yellow arrow pointed us back from this edge on another path that paralleled the stream. We climbed steeply in the rich, mulch-scented shade of old trees and saw no one.

Maria wondered aloud whether we were lost, but each time she spoke we seemed to find a new marker. We paused for water. Gnats besieged us. We continued. Prickly vines grabbed at our bare calves and made them itch. Maria said she was tired. I chirped cheerfully to keep us moving and to hide my own discouragement.

We passed an obelisk that lay fallen on its side. As the afternoon wore on we passed no more yellow arrows or obelisks. I wondered aloud whether we would be sleeping outdoors. We kept to the most obvious path and it led us to a wooded ridge where we heard highway traffic far below us. The guidebook was packed away, but I remembered that road and path met again before the summit, where we would walk a short way along the highway again. Traffic sounds faded and disappeared as we continued up the ridge.

Maria saw power lines back down the ravine toward the creek. The guidebook had described walking beneath high-voltage lines near the summit. I stumbled, then ran, almost falling down the hillside to the clearing beneath the lines and headed up hill.

"Wait for me, Dad," Maria yelled.

We fell into step slogging through grass beneath the humming lines. We followed the line for much longer than I'd expected from the guidebook. We climbed a couple of hundred feet more and emerged at the road. Our book described this stone chapel and summit. I converted the altitude sign to feet and announced to Maria that we had just climbed 3,600 feet. Wisps of fog from the far side cooled us.

Two signs pointed toward Roncesvalles—to the right down the highway or left down a path.

The guidebook had cautioned cyclists about the very steep road. "No more traffic for us today," I said. Had I looked at our map, I would have seen Roncesvalles a steep ten-minute walk down the road, and seen that the trail was an hour and half longer. It was six o'clock.

High gray fog faded to bluish dusk. The path's hard-packed clay felt good underfoot. We saw and felt our way down and down as it grew dark. The path joined a level roadway by a creek. There was no sign, but remembering that this path had forked left from the highway, we turned right. The short grass we felt underfoot was worn from pilgrims walking here regularly. This must be the right way. We still saw no one.

Around the base of a hill, we saw the monastery looming almost black against the thin burnished hint of a sunset. The great clustered building had no lights we could see, but we knew. "Roncesvalles! We made it!" **D**

. . . . . .

WE WERE BONE-TIRED and wanted food and beds, but we couldn't find a door. We had been alone all day and we were still alone, with darkness falling fast.

Walking toward the dark wall, we saw twilight through a broad passage, and went in. Through the passage we emerged outdoors again between two high stone walls. To our left two or three low windows and the stained glass higher up marked the church. To our right a stairway cut through three stories of sheer stonework to an outdoor terrace. We heard laughter above. Facing the terrace, the monastery ran perpendicular to the church. Above us the two buildings formed a courtyard.

People stood talking brightly. Had they walked here too? I felt road-weary, gray, dusty and old. Someone slipped past us into the church. Chant and a glimpse of golden, shimmering candles and sculpted saints escaped. The pilgrims' mass! I wanted to go in.

"Not yet," Maria said over her shoulder. She was talking with a stranger. I heard her thank him as he headed to the main gate. "Going to the pilgrims' dinner at the hotel," she explained. "We're too late to sign up."

"What will we eat?" I asked.

"We'll find something."

"Shall we go to mass?"

"No," Maria decreed, "beds first, then dinner." She started up the outdoor stairs. I climbed two at a time and overtook her. After the afternoon's rough climb the steady rhythm of the smooth stairs felt surprisingly good. Fifty steps up, we found more people talking on the stone terrace. "This looks like the first day of high school," Maria whispered.

"Or an Escher painting," I replied, glancing at the stone face of this building designed for people who knew where they were going. A young pilgrim nodded us toward an unmarked door. Just inside, a noisy group of young people stopped eating and offered us, "upstairs," "more stairs," "lots of stairs," in various languages.

We climbed another flight. This time a "*Refugio*" sign and an arrow sent us through an old wooden door and more stairs and another door and to a harried, balding man behind a desk. The monk!

He broke off lecturing three young people on pilgrim manners to hurry them up another stairway. When he returned to his desk, I offered him our letter from the bishop. "No," he said, "*No necesita,*" handing us forms to fill out.

The guestmaster was too tired to look at our letter.

Maria saw my disappointment. She took the letters from me and gave them to the monk. "My father wants you to look at our letters."

"*Bueno,*" he said, extending an open hand. He glanced at them without reading, folded them quickly, and gave them back. "*Bueno,*" he said again, and pointed to his forms. He asked for our passports and copied numbers from them into a book which he had us sign. Then he produced two accordion-folded papers the same size and thickness as the passports. I recognized our *credencias*. He stamped each with two different stamps and gave one to Maria and one to me.

"*Muchas gracias,*" I said as warmly as I could.

"*De nada,*" he replied. I tried to remind myself that "It's nothing," in Spanish really means "You're welcome."

We followed him up the last flight to a renovated loft. Heavy wood rafter beams and tiny window dormers appeared old enough, but everything else was brand new: windows in the dormers, doors, concrete floor, and one white tile bathroom with a dozen stall toilets and as

· · · · · ·

many stall showers. Most of the fifty or so double bunks already had sleeping bags on top and bottom. The old man pointed us to an empty bunk close to the door. I looked at my *credencia*, one stamp for our starting point, and one for this first night in a *refugio*.

"Come on, Dad. I need some dinner," Maria said. **D**

Erosion
· · · · ·

WHEN WE GOT UP, everyone else was already gone. Neither of us had set an alarm clock. I reminded Maria that we were actually a whole day's experience ahead of everyone who had come to Roncesvalles by bus. "But they're ahead of us for beds tonight," she said.

I wanted to see the monastery's pilgrim museum. Maria was glad it was closed so we could get started. I suggested we eat first. We sat in the shelter of Charlemagne's battle monument and shivered through our cold breakfast of bread, cheese and nuts. Maria stamped against the cold, impatient that so many were ahead of us. "Come on, Dad. Let's go." I assured her we would walk fast enough to pass many of them.

We checked our maps and left Roncesvalles by the paved road. At a *crucero*, a medieval pilgrim's cross placed as a small shrine and way-marker, we left the highway for the replanted forest. The morning's walk was easy, like a National Park nature walk, strolling briskly along a graded gravel path through new trees and undergrowth. The path felt and sounded good underfoot. I pushed us along through forest and meadow and a prosperous, stone-paved village, white plaster, fresh paint, and brightly varnished shutters.

At the next village, we found an open *tienda* and stopped to replenish our groceries with fresh-baked bread, *serrano* ham, nuts and juice. I wanted to find somewhere for coffee. Maria

· · · · ·

wanted to press on. She was having trouble with my pace and wanted to walk a little slower but stop less.

We followed the Camino out of the farming valley, up into wilder woods. After a brief ascent we started down and continued mostly down until the day's end, down the foothills of the Pyrenees, leaving the rest of Europe behind.

Sometime after noon we had our first encounter with the old Camino. The erosion surprised me. A thousand winters had stripped the skin of soil from the path and bared the mountain's skeleton, rock slabs tilted on end by shifting continents. We had to place each foot carefully on the stone slabs' jagged edges, using our walking sticks to keep balance. A misstep would mean a cut knee, a twisted ankle or a fall off the path into the thorny undergrowth.

I knew from the day before what to do with my stick. On rocky or uneven ground it revealed the shape of the terrain. Walking down steep or rocky hills it offered practical comfort. When I misstepped, the stick helped me catch my balance.

I thought of the millions of pilgrims who had walked before us. Saint Francis had walked across these stones. I tried to guess how many hundreds or thousands of our English, Scottish, Welsh, French and German ancestors had walked this exact path.

Maria didn't want to talk about my musings. She was thinking about the fifty or a hundred people who walked ahead of us from Roncesvalles. The next two *refugios* had only room for three dozen people in total.

We overtook a group of half a dozen pilgrims and wished them "*Buen Camino,*" as we pressed on. "Six more beds," I whispered to Maria. We passed another pair. "See," I said, "we'll be fine," thinking to myself, "We're winning." When we stopped to cool off, take a drink of water, and adjust our packs, the same six people passed us, waving just as cheerily as we had. "Damn," I said under my breath and then caught myself. Was this a foot race or a pilgrimage? **D**

THE AFTERNOON WORE ON and our progress was very slow, but I had invented a Saying For Pilgrims to deliver us from anxious competition: "The other pilgrims are your friends."

I explained to Maria that seeing others as pilgrims just like us would make us, in faith and good hope, give up the foot race and simply pray, or wish, or intend hot showers and good beds for all at the end of the day.

"Fine, Dad. I hope you're right about that," she said. Too focused on a shower to hear my discovery, I thought. We kept walking. I repeated it quietly to myself like a mantra, "The other pilgrims are our friends." I planned to write it down when we stopped. It would be the first of my discovered spiritual principles of pilgrimage.

I fit my mantra to the natural rhythm of walking. With a stick's accent, my walking rhythm became four/four (right/left, right/left), four footsteps to each stick click or plod.

With my right hand resting on top of the stick, a natural rounded knob, I could make a tiny wrist motion that swung the stick forward, pendulum-like, until it floated for a moment in the air. This coordinated the stick to every other stride of my right foot. As I developed an ease with my stick, out of curiosity I asked Maria to try trading sticks. We each found the other's stick ill-fitted and preferred our own.

The stick had begun to feel like a supportive, healing friend. When my shoulder joints began to ache from the simple weight of my arms, I lay the stick across my neck like a yoke and draped both arms over it. "You look like some kind of *penitente*, Dad," Maria said. My weary joints didn't care. "Try it," I said. She did. "Wow, that really opens up all the tightness in my back."

Our guidebook told us to look for the old pilgrims' hostel on the ridge. It would have an identifying sign. The trail was the only access to this large, medieval stone building with

. . . . . .

its slate roof intact. When we found it, Maria didn't want to stop. I said I'd be quick. Coming into the dark, I saw nothing but heard something large. Huge, faintly luminous white shapes rose and shifted in the darkness.

Finally my eyes adjusted enough to see what my nose should have told me, that I had upset half a dozen sleeping cows. They were struggling to their feet, jostling, pushing, and angrily moo-ing toward me. Their hooves squished the thick, dungy mud. This was no place to soak up the prayers and voices of medieval pilgrims. Maria was outside waiting impatiently. "Enough, Dad?" she asked. "Plenty," I replied.

The ridge we followed ran parallel to a river. Our map placed the closer refugio, Zubirí, just across the Río Arga. We kept seeing towns across the river and passing them. Where was Zubirí? We walked much slower than we had in the morning. Both of us had blisters.

Eventually the path turned down off the ridge. Here the stone, laid flat and polished by human footsteps, was smooth and slick. We were relieved to get to level ground beside the river and walk on hard-packed earth. Soon we came to the stone-arched medieval pilgrim's bridge. An arrow pointed us to Zubirí's *refugio*. I was hobbling on sore feet, annoyed that Maria seemed to be walking better than me. If Zubirí was full, we could remind ourselves that "the other pilgrims are our friends," and press on. Daylight would last another two hours. Perhaps we could actually keep walking. **D**

Clean Start
· · · · · ·

IT WAS NEARLY 7 P.M. when we crossed the old pilgrim's bridge into Zubirí. The town was small, a few blocks long with a bar and a grocery. We walked down the main street trying to find the *refugio*, failing and then retracing our steps. It felt ridiculous to be lost in a place

· · · · · ·

so small. My legs protested useless wandering at the end of the day. Finally a young boy pointed us to a sixties-era school building we had passed twice.

We entered through a side door of the narrow one-story building. With the extra heft of my backpack, I struggled to get through the door. I bounced off the doorframe like a pinball. Once in the door my bag kept catching on things. My walking stick turned clumsy and awkward. I felt like a parody of a real pilgrim.

I looked around. With bunk beds replacing desks, the *refugio* seemed more like a makeshift disaster shelter than an ancient place of hospitality. The walls were stripped of any evidence of school. The bulletin board had a note posted about hours of operation and cost, about two dollars. There was no one to stamp our *credencias*.

Five or six pilgrims lay quietly on their beds, vacantly staring. A few heads lifted, looked indifferently in our direction, and then turned away. This is what an opium den must be like, I thought to myself. Dad and I whispered to one another as we chose bunks.

I took off my pack. Without the weight on my back I floated, disconnected from the ground.

A woman appeared in the doorway. Her easy stride told me she was not a pilgrim. She had come to stamp our *credencias* and collect the fee. I went to get my money and *credencias* from the bottom of my bag. Bending down and pulling at things in my pack interrupted the euphoric floating with stiff pain.

Had to think, things to be done. We both took off our boots and socks. Dad lay down. I looked at my feet. They were slightly swollen, pink and moist with sweat. I had a small blister on my toe. I wanted a shower.

I took my things into the bathroom. The room had only two showerheads and some sinks. I was alone. I stripped down to my flip-flops and turned on the shower. The water ran cold, but the strong pressure beat the dirt off me. There was no lock on the door or curtain for the shower, and the only window to the small room would not completely close. Outside two boys played soccer. There was nothing to stop them from looking at me. I didn't care. I put on my fresh clothes. I felt better, and very tired.

Dad took his turn in the shower. With only a little daylight left I decided not to wait for him, and started the washing. In the deep sink it was hard keep the water from splashing me where I leaned against the rim. It felt good. Dad came out and did his wash too. We hung our things to dry on the jungle gym. We ate our dinner in the *refugio*. With our clean clothes drying, and a full stomach, I felt ready for a new day. *M*

An Ordinary Pilgrim
. . . . .

NEXT AFTERNOON IN ARRE, the Brazilian we had met in Zubirí said the *refugio* would open at four. She was resting by the door in the shade of the arched porch. We slid our packs off and sat beside her. The stone floor and walls felt cool. The path we had missed crossed a broad stone footbridge that led right into this porch. I could just hear the river's whisper.

A Fiat's gearbox screamed, as the driver downshifted and screeched to a halt before us. He leapt out, leaving the engine running, and marched towards us, flushed red and sweating profusely. As he came he tugged his black shirt closed, buttoned it, and inserted a white clerical collar in its slot. He stepped over us and pounded on the door, calling loudly in Italian for the guestmaster.

A monk in khakis and T-shirt opened the door to say in measured Spanish that the guestmaster was in France.

But—the priest insisted—twenty students! He had reserved months ago! There had to be a record of it! His Italian came faster, punctuated by German mutterings.

. . . . .

I watched this brother priest with an empty feeling in the pit of my stomach. Did I act like this?

The monk said he had to deal with the waiting pilgrims first. Then he would do his best.

"*Tenemos reservaciones!*"

"*Refugios* do not take reservations," the monk replied gently. "First spaces go to pilgrims with packs, then to those on horseback, then cyclists, and last to pilgrims with vehicle support." He pointed to the Fiat, filled to the ceiling with backpacks.

The priest spluttered a protest.

"*Un momento*," the monk said as he motioned the Brazilian, Maria and me inside.

The stone room felt cool. A large Virgin of Guadalupe on the wall matched the image on my T-shirt. He stamped at our *credencias*. "*Padre y hija?*" he asked me. "Father and daughter?"

"*Sí.*" It was too complicated to explain that I was a priest, too.

He led us back out past the priest glowering in the Fiat, past the old church to a heavy door in an old building back from the river.

"This was our first building," he explained, showing us into the *refugio*. It had been recently remodeled from a medieval pilgrims' hospital. Icon prints of Rublev's Savior and the Holy Trinity hung in the hall. I wanted to tell him the same icons hung on our wall at home, but didn't.

"For the father and daughter," he said, opening the curtained doorway to *refugio*'s one double room. He began laying mattresses out on the common room and dormitory floors. People kept coming and coming.

Finally he went to find the priest and his students, twenty or so college-age young men and women, all as long as the priest was round. He led them to a dormitory room at the end of the hall. The students wore colored kerchiefs around their necks like boy scouts. We heard them settling in as we finished our wash.

· · · · · ·

Outside a black dog lay in the heat watching me hang my socks and underclothes. The priest stormed out, and interrupted the monk, who was welcoming two bicycle pilgrims. "No hot water!" The dog looked at him quizzically. "I need a classroom to tell my students about the Camino!" The dog lay his head down and closed his eyes.

"So many people showering," the monk agreed, "uses up the hot water." The dormitory would do for the class.

We went out to sit in the monastery's garden to eat our supper of bread, fruit and canned squid. A mother cat and her kittens watched and mewed at us. The monk led the cyclists past us and opened the door to the church, apologizing that he had no more mattresses. Thanking him for the shelter, they said their air mattresses would be plenty. **D**

Shadow Fears

· · · · ·

I WENT TO BED RESTLESS and slept little. The German priest and his group worried me. We had no tent, and depended on hotels if a *refugio* was full. We were only six kilometers from Pamplona. Crowds, who had come for the running of the bulls, had taken every hotel bed within a hundred miles. Pamplona's *refugio* had been closed to keep out fraudulent pilgrims. Cizur Menor, the next *refugio* on our route, was closed for remodeling. This left Puente la Reina, where pilgrims from Jaca converged on our Camino. Puente la Reina couldn't possibly house us all.

I began a dangerous game of counting. The Germans took at least twenty beds, the two closed *refugios* another thirty. How many more pilgrims would join us from Jaca? I imagined our arrival, no beds and no place to sleep. We would have to settle for a doorway. Maybe

· · · · ·

this would fit into some medieval fantasy of Dad's but I only saw a newspaper headline. "GIRL AND FATHER ATTACKED IN DOORWAY … DAD PROTESTS 'BUT ALL PILGRIMS ARE OUR FRIENDS!'"

To even get to Puente la Reina we would have to walk twenty-nine kilometers, our longest walk yet. I decided to wake Dad. *M*

• • •

Arre was still. We passed through knots of sleepy people waiting for an early bus. Despite San Fermín, they were dressed for work. I wondered how the men in their jackets and ties would bear the day's heat.

A painted yellow arrow pointed us down an alley and out into a glowing dust cloud, red with brake lights, where traffic lurched through road construction. Everything was torn up, not just pavement but sidewalk and our yellow markers.

We asked three girls at an unfinished bus stop for directions. "Over there," one said, pointing beyond torn-up roadway to the deep darkness. "Try over there."

We walked toward oncoming headlights, trying to watch the broken ground. Shadows bounced and wheeled with the traffic. Could the girl have meant this small street that led into deep gloom? It looked to me to be the kind of street that a good father would tell his daughter to avoid.

Maria spotted a yellow arrow on a sidewalk fragment. We looked for a second arrow, but the rest of the sidewalk was gone. Maria said if we found no yellow arrows, we'd just head for the center of Pamplona. I agreed reluctantly, imagining how to use my stick as a weapon if someone tried to jump us.

Our guidebook had noted that road construction would detour us past Pamplona's city dump. The stink of trash, dust and diesel fuel confirmed we were on the right track. For several hundred meters we walked beside a concrete wall, telling each other how glad we were it wasn't hotter.

Beyond the wall we entered a ghost town of warehouses, abandoned buildings, and the occasional wrought iron gate. We walked quietly and spoke softly. I was listening. There were no streetlights at all. One growling, snapping dog followed us the length of his chain link fence. More warehouses. A few lost cottages surrounded by trees. Unexplained noises. And more snarling growling dogs. We walked in an adrenaline-soaked haze.

I recited to myself, "Thy rod and thy staff, they comfort me." The staff in the psalm was my trusty stick. I swung it and wished we'd done more stick practice in aikido.

We were approaching the city. Steel bars over every door and window replaced the dogs. Who slept inside these silent, barricaded houses and what dangers did they fear in these streets? **D**

• • •

I tried to warn Dad we were now entering a Big City. Our clothes marked us as foreigners, and with our backpacks we were slow-moving targets for thieves, muggers, and pickpockets. Dad nodded, lost in his own thoughts. "He doesn't know," I told myself. I, on the other hand, did know. I knew because a little more than a year before, I had been robbed on the street in Madrid.

Sherry would object. It was she, after all, who was robbed. I was just the bystander, the stupid one who had insisted on taking the subway and bus (instead of a cab) to the airport. It was cold that early morning as we dragged our suitcases through the streets of Madrid. Sherry, the savvy New Yorker, knew someone followed us. I remained oblivious.

As we walked down the steps into the subway, two enormous hands emerged from the shadows, reaching for Sherry. Thinking they would grope her, I screamed her name. As she turned they stopped just short of her body, grabbing her small backpack. With terrifying speed these hands pulled the bag up and away from her, snapped the straps off, and disappeared. I don't remember a face, only open hands reaching for her.

I couldn't escape the feeling of déjà vu. I looked around. The dark streets began to fill with people. Was it safer now than when we were alone? Our packs were too heavy to just grab and run with. My money and documents lay hidden deep in my bag, out of the reach of an ordinary pickpocket. The thief would be driven to threaten us. I pushed tragic headlines out of my head. "This is it," I thought to myself as we neared the city's center. It was up to me to keep alert. We passed through a small park where revelers lay sleeping on the grass. Dad had no idea what we were about to enter. *M*

Temptation
. . . . .

IT WAS NEARING 5:30 A.M. as we walked into the fortress of old Pamplona. I clenched my hands tightly around my shoulder straps. I knew what was coming. I knew the Spanish fiesta. The sane had retreated to the safety of home by 4 a.m. At this hour we would find only troublesome drunks. "It's crazy," my Spanish friends had warned me. The runners invested a full night to work themselves into drunken arrogant bravado before the bulls entered the streets at 8 a.m.

The Pamplona I see in our guidebook is quite beautiful. A classic Spanish city of cobblestone streets and medieval buildings, well maintained save for horn-height scrape marks. This is not what I see now; this is not the city in the photos. That morning we walked into a city under siege, revelers holding it captive. They pushed up against us, danced around us, hung out of buildings above us and slept on curbs below us. From open bar windows peo-

. . . . .

ple and music overflowed into the street, blurring the difference between inside and out. This wasn't a crowd contained in a flat plain, but an amorphous mob inhabiting every level of the city.

Only dress unified this chaos. The mob wore white, set off by blood-red sashes at the waist and matching red bandanas. Everyone, even mannequins in the windows, wore this white and red uniform. Strobe lights from the bars made the white blaze and the red burn. The sky hid human faces with its somber dark blue, protecting all's anonymity. Our pilgrim clothes in dusty tan and beige screamed, "We are not one of you."

Our presence was unwelcome, but we could not hide. We were too awake, too alert, and too sober. Worst of all, we moved with direction through a crowd of drifters. We dodged and pushed through the red-white mass, desperately looking for the yellow markers that could lead us out of the city.

Noise saturated everything. Glass crunching underfoot, a thousand voices speaking at once, and the unending rhythm of club music. I felt the sound push through my chest, interrupting and confusing the rhythm of my heartbeat and breathing. The party's own joyous momentum was gone. We were surrounded by the defiant, proudly staying past the hour of good fun. This night they readied themselves to risk death in the name of tradition.

Some people yelled and pointed at us, one girl made a wildly uncoordinated effort to trip Dad. The crowd kept threatening to separate us.

I felt shame at my familiarity with this scene. And yet part of me desperately wanted to drop my bag, tie a red sash around my waist and have a beer. "We walked into a Bruegel painting," I said to Dad. "Temptations of the Pilgrims."

The street filled with the smell of cooking meat. A man my father's age, dressed in brown, pushed fat sausages across a hot grill. They sizzled and hissed at us. Suddenly I was very hungry. We bought two sandwiches, juicy sausage on good bread. Like the best temptations, they were delicious and came at an unusually high price.

By now dawn broke as the Camino led us out through a large park to the edge of the city. The sky burned Technicolor blue. The park was littered with trash, broken bottles and sleeping drunks. Despite this, it was beautiful. I relaxed the grip on my shoulder straps and let out a sigh. *M*

Black Dog
· · · · ·

THE COLD WIND SWEPT US along rattled fields of chattering wheat kernels. After getting through Pamplona so early, we hoped to reach Puente la Reina ahead of our pilgrim friends. Wind massed a storm behind us. Dark clouds over Pamplona hid the sunrise. Ahead of us shadowy mountains rose beyond the wheat fields. Puente la Reina lay somewhere over those mountains.

Maria had seen an eleven-year-old walking slowly with his father. Where would they find a room tonight?

The black dog from Arre bounded up, greeting us with a nudge. As he fell in alongside us wagging his tail, a lean man strode beside to join him. "So, you have met my dog," the man said in French-accented English. We moved faster to match his pace.

"By the clothesline in Arre," I replied.

He laughed a little. "We saw you there, but we did not speak. My dog is not allowed in Spanish *refugios*. Last night there was also no room for him."

"It was certainly crowded," I said.

"That Italian priest and his pupils," the Frenchman said.

· · · · ·

"German, I thought."

"Of course," the Frenchman smiled, "a German."

"So your dog slept outside?" Maria interjected.

"He is a good dog. He sleeps where I tell him. In France he slept at the foot of my bed."

"So you began in France?" I asked.

"Oh, this year only at Saint Jean, but last summer I walked in France from Vézelay. I walk every summer. This summer we finish to Santiago."

"We began at Saint Jean," Maria said, "three days ago."

"Ah, where we began day before last," he said. "But I see you got an early start this morning."

"Four-thirty," Maria said.

"Very early then," he seemed a little surprised at the hour.

"And you?" I asked.

"Just after six."

An hour and a half after us! So, at this pace, he had walked from Roncesvalles to Arre in one day. We were moving faster as we walked with him. It felt good.

The simplicity of his conversation carried us along like his practiced, effortless stride. He said he was a school teacher and walked every summer. He asked questions about us. I enjoyed his curiosity and interest. The school teacher was teaching us how to walk, his words and walk gently reshaping ours.

"So French *refugios* allow dogs?" I asked.

"We have almost no *refugios*, but with a letter from your priest, homes along the way will take you in and give you dinner and a bed. Perhaps you give them something in thanks."

"Do you carry water for the dog?"

· · · · · ·

"No. He finds puddles and ponds by the Camino. He sniffs first and sometimes will not drink. I suppose he knows what is good and what is not."

"Does he ever have trouble keeping up?"

"I stop in the afternoon for a little nap, and he rests. Then we walk again until dark. Did you see how he ran ahead to meet you? He runs from group to group trying to herd them together. So he walks far longer each day than I do." **D**

Frenchman Sensei

· · · · · ·

FOR AN HOUR AND A HALF we walked the fastest pace we would sustain for the whole Camino. The black dog bounded ahead to greet each little clump of pilgrims we were overtaking. No one passed us, though about half a mile ahead, two people kept our same pace. The dog ignored them.

I told our friend I was hoping to walk the Camino again with my wife and other children.

"My wife would never do this," he said, "but she understands I need it." He paused, adding in French, "And it's better than a mistress." I laughed.

"I think my wife would do this," I said, responding in French and forgetting to translate.

He went back to English. "My older son won't walk this with me," he said. "Once we were close, but now he is sixteen, so to him, I know and understand nothing. My daughter loves me but she will not walk. My younger son, he wants to walk. He is eight. Next year perhaps, while we still enjoy one another."

Maria asked in Spanish whether we could speak Spanish. He laughed, "I can only say, 'He is a good dog,' and 'He will sleep where you want.'"

· · · · · ·

We passed another group of pilgrims. He asked in English, "How did you prepare for this walk?"

Maria described hiking in Massachusetts.

I admitted my feet hurt because I had not walked enough in preparation, but it seemed that daily aikido gave me plenty of wind and endurance.

"Aikido!" he exclaimed with delight. "My son and I practice daily. It is the one place we are still together. When did you begin practicing?"

"Sixteen years ago."

"I practice too," Maria added.

"Ah." He paused and then asked me, "*Sho-dan*?" (Japanese for "black belt.")

"Fifth degree," I replied.

He stopped walking. "Then I bow to you, Sensei," he said folding his hands, bowing from the waist. He resumed walking, but the pace was slowed. We were quiet. Why had I told him the ranking? "Yes" would have been enough.

Maria whispered that she was thirsty and needed to rest. My feet hurt too, and I wanted to see if moleskin would help. I told our friend we were taking a break. He wished us well. He and the dog strode on, quickly overtaking the pair who had held so steady ahead of us. He disappeared over a hill. Our hearty pace had been a compromise for him.

I asked Maria if I had said too much about my black belt. "He asked," she replied distantly, "and it's true." I wished I had returned his bow and called him "Sensei," teacher. **D**

· · · · · ·

THE WIND BLEW COLD on our backs as we walked up the ridge. I had been feeling lonely and abandoned by Dad in his conversation with the Frenchman. I wondered if he had noticed how he had walked ahead of me to keep up with the man's pace, or how much they had spoken in French, a language I don't understand. It was just the two of us again, so I said nothing.

The path ran a long diagonal ascent across the steep face. The mountain was bare, heavy wind discouraging any real vegetation. We walked under a gray sky toward the summit that was crowned by a line of modern windmills. Standing fifty or sixty feet high, some spun furiously, others remained ominously still. We stopped to take pictures, each pretending to be Don Quixote, wielding our walking sticks like lances at the whirling blades high above us.

The wind burned the back of my legs as it swept off the plain and rushed up the ridge. Rain smeared down out of the sky toward Pamplona, distant but still visible across the valley. We would have to walk quickly to keep ahead of this weather. The wind pushed hard on my hat. I snapped up both my brims to keep it from flying off. We kept walking.

We approached a pair of pilgrims about my age. As we got closer I saw a towel hanging off the back of the taller one's pack. The towel had worked loose from the straps of his pack, and now snapped back and forth in the wind. It never touched his legs or arms, so he walked unaware he was about to lose it. I ran toward them. "The towel!" I yelled, first in Spanish and then in English. The two pilgrims stopped as Dad and I caught up. The pair were from Poland and spoke good English but minimal Spanish. The four of us set to fixing the problem. The taller Pole, who now had his pack off his back, tried to push the towel back under the straps, but the wind kept snapping it out of place. "It won't stay," he said, frustrated.

"Safety pins!" I said, as quickly as I thought it.

. . . . . .

I had many safety pins in my pack but had yet to use any of them. Days before in Zubirí, a middle-aged Spanish woman who was walking the pilgrimage for the third time expounded on the subtleties of pilgrimming. Puffing away on cigarette after cigarette, she showed us, the novice pilgrims in the *refugio*, her old *credencias* and told us of places to stay and things to do on the route. "You will need these," she said in a raspy, low voice as she poured a handful of safety pins on the table. "These are very good." She did not explain why.

Advice, the currency of the pilgrimage, was abundant and free. Everyone knew the precise single ingredient that would prevent disaster. Ear plugs, extra shoelaces, a pocketknife, a sewing kit, rubber bands, white cotton thread, Zip-lock bags; we carried these items not knowing why, hoping that in each disaster we would learn.

"Safety pins!" I repeated. The two Polish pilgrims looked at me perplexed. Thinking it was a language problem I told Dad to get out the pins from my pack, still on my back. They looked at the pins and ran them between their fingers. I took one out of the shorter pilgrim's hand, opened and closed it. "To fasten the towel," I said. He smiled and nodded. We quickly attached the towel to his friend's pack. He looked at the towel, now firmly fixed on the pack. "These pins. They are good!" *M*

Learning to Sleep

BACK ON OUR FIRST DAY, I had feared that darkness would strand us, forcing us to sleep in the woods. I was still carrying this worry. Wondering where we would sleep the next night haunted my dreams.

In Zubirí, I had pushed my plastic earplugs firmly in and felt the odd discomfort of pressure in my ears as I heard distant, muffled sounds from people nearby. I had these earplugs because a friend of a friend had walked the Camino and insisted we'd want them. Lying on a saggy top bunk, I drifted into fitful sleep, imagining the hard nights ahead. I woke shaking in the dark, still in a dream that wouldn't let go. Had my earplug become an insect that had eaten its way into my ear canal? Was I bleeding from my ear and was I going to bleed to death? I felt my ear and the pillow, found them dry, and went back to sleep.

In Trinidad de Arre, I slept my first real pilgrim sleep, a sleep sufficient to the glory and pain of the day, a satisfied sleep of recovery and restoration. After that night I slept like a hard-working, contented farmer, glad to close my eyes with the dark and glad to open them again before light.

Puente la Reina was our last night bunking above and below. We had both discovered how much easier early morning packing was from the lower bunk, so we began taking side by side lowers, which put Maria in better reach to nudge me when I snored.

Most *refugios* would be smaller than Puente la Reina, with rooms not so tightly packed. Typically a room slept eight people in four double-deck bunks. There were no pillows, so I made one each night by rolling up my towel and wrapping a clean T-shirt around it. This make-shift pillow and a good mattress made for a good night's sleep.

Each night I would ask Maria to tell our roommates that I might snore. I loved hearing her say "*roncar*," a verb whose rolling "rrr" captures the startling sound it names. She said that if my snoring didn't wake her, anyone else should feel free to nudge me to a different, quieter position. She only had to wake me a few times. I snored less on the pilgrimage than I usually do.

But back to Puente la Reina. We and seventy-nine other people shared a room packed full of triple-decker bunks. When we arrived that afternoon, I stretched out my sleeping bag on a middle bunk and lay on top of it. The simple comfort of a good firm bed made up for crowding and lack of privacy. I napped to the sound of rain on the roof. Back in the bunk after supper, I decided to sleep without earplugs. I woke once listening to the peaceful breathing of eighty decent people who were as tired and as glad to rest as I was. I closed my eyes again in peace. **D**

Blisters

. . . . . .

AFTER OUR SECOND DAY I walked on blisters all the way to Santiago. I didn't get blisters on my heels, but on the bottoms of my feet. Sometimes the pads of my heels, the balls of my feet and the tips of my toes hurt so much that I feared I would have to stop. Sometimes the blisters were only a forgettable annoyance.

Most mornings I woke anticipating the day's walk, happily padding around barefoot as we washed up and packed. But putting my boots on, lacing them up, and standing, awakened the pain. First steps in the boots, muscles and nerves mindlessly sought whatever awkward walk might keep pressure off the worst blisters. Sometimes I rolled out onto my ankles, sometimes put my feet down softly and tiptoed, sometimes placed each flat-footed step lifting my toes inside the boots so that sore, tender toe-pads wouldn't touch down.

Fearing pulled muscles and joints, I would stop and say, "Maria, I've got to make a slow start this morning." Invariably she responded with a patient, "Don't worry about it, Dad." Trying not to gasp when it hurt, I consciously measured my breathing to keep it even and deep, and tried to shape a natural walk.

Gradually my body would find a more flowing way to move. My feet didn't stop hurting, but I tasted the morning's fresh air and the huge privilege of another day of walking.

. . . . . .

Looking forward to the day's scents and sounds, and feeling the pleasure my hips and thigh muscles took in a smooth flowing walk made the hurt seem smaller. Little by little my stride lengthened, until afternoon.

Afternoons I plodded. When I longed for rest, it was work to keep focus. I had to walk past the subtle, frightening pain of a new blister just forming, or the sharp pain of an old one filling up again. I protested rests. Starting after a rest was as hard as beginning in the morning, but without the fresh energy or resolve. The last steps of the afternoon were the worst. **D**

Estella
· · · · · ·

BY LATE AFTERNOON of our fifth day my right knee ached, my hips were sore, and my walking had become an angry stomping to the silent mantra of WHY … AREN'T … WE … THERE … YET? Just as I wonder if we had missed our destination, the Camino turned sharply and Estella opened out in front of us. We followed a gentle river into the city. The afternoon sun gilded the water and lightened my mood. Medieval buildings and beaux-arts apartments lined the streets. Mercifully the *refugio* was just across the bridge, near the Romanesque palace of the king of Navarra.

The *hospitalero* showed us to a dorm room on the second floor. After showering we took our dirty clothes downstairs to wash. The large, red-tiled patio behind the *refugio* was filled with pilgrims talking of the day's progress. I took my sweaty, dirty clothes to the big outdoor sinks. I was about to submerge my shirt in the cold water when I heard from above me. "*Oye!* The good soap is next to the other sink!" I glanced up. From the window of a house overlooking the patio, an old Spanish woman waved me to the soap. "Not there! Put

· · · · · ·

it on the other line!" she yelled to another pilgrim hanging out a wet shirt. More pilgrims came, more directions. Watching Dad hang out our socks, she yelled to me "Hey, in America, men do the washing?"

As we were finishing hanging our laundry, a group of barefoot pilgrims gathered around an old man sitting on a step at the other end of the patio. On the ground beside him he laid out surgical tape, scissors, bandages and two small jars of green mud. A Spanish woman pointed to my feet and said in English, "He will heal your blisters." We watched him rub the sticky green muck on each raw sore. He bandaged each slathered blister and sealed it with surgical tape.

We stood quietly, slightly away from the group, our shoes still on. Anyone who could tell us if this stuff really worked was a couple of days ahead of us on the Camino. "I don't think Mom would like this," Dad whispered to me. She would worry about infection.

We left the foot shaman as he treated Nick, a Canadian we had met a few days before. I still wanted to believe in the magic of the green mud, but I wasn't the one with all the blisters.

Walking through Estella's cobblestoned streets I looked for a souvenir of the city. We passed a shop filled with hand-bound leather journals, beautiful but heavy. Another place sold handsome carved walking sticks, but that would mean abandoning my own. I had resigned myself to postcards, when pilgrim shells, laid out in a glass case by some cheap pens, caught my eye. I had seen people with these white scallops, the traditional badge of a pilgrim, attached to backpacks and worn on a string as a necklace. We bought two and put them on immediately.

Armed with the name of the city's oldest tavern and restaurant, we asked a local woman for directions. The sudden sound of clapping, flutes, and drums interrupted her vague instructions. "Ah, yes. The festival," she said, motioning behind her. Forgetting our hunger,

· · · · · ·

my sore knee, and Dad's blisters we darted down the street. "This way," Dad yelled as he took a quick turn down an alley. We stepped out into a parade of musicians in medieval dress singing and marching through the city.

They stopped to act a medieval story of adultery on the pilgrimage to a medieval tune. Another stop produced a motet. Feeling quite hungry, I motioned to Dad to separate from the group and eat. "Let's follow them for one more song," he said.

Just as my attention waned with my growing hunger, I looked up. They were singing an old song about the restaurant we were looking for, and there above us was its awning. We returned from our dinner happy, tired, and full of good food and wine. I fell asleep to the music of Handel drifting in from the street outside. *M*

A Day of Hospitality

. . . . .

WE BEGAN THE MORNING by stretching. Maria's knee was sore and stiff, but we were optimistic about it healing as we walked. Our way was hilly, and she borrowed my staff on the downhill. Walking with two staffs eased the strain on her knee.

In Irucha, just an hour or so out, we paused for a sip of wine from the famed wine fountain, a little faucet and basin in the wall of a *bodega*. A sign reminded the locals that this wine was for pilgrims. Maria and I each drank a swallow from our new pilgrim shells. It was good.

It was getting warm again. The hills were golden-dry like California. I was worried about Maria's sore knee, and we agreed to stretch before and after each rest. Helping one another along was an unexpected part of the pilgrimage.

We walked a dirt farm road. Beyond a hill we found our way blocked by sheep, a shepherd and his dogs crossing them from one pasture to another. We waited. After the flock

. . . . .

crossed, we passed the shepherd's truck, parked in the roadway to shade a ewe and her new-born lamb.

The Camino left the dirt road for a narrow path of packed earth through tall golden straw. We walked into a dense bank of wild roses, a flowery wall to our right and left, starting an explosion of butterflies, flapping hundreds of wings that stirred the sun-warmed scent of the roses. We talked happily, walking through golden hills. A cultivated field of lavender, a purple-blue square tucked into the wild hillside, dazzled like sky fallen to earth.

We arrived in Los Arcos in time for a shower and a leisurely late lunch. We wandered through town. I enjoyed walking in my sandals. "Los Arcos looks like a farm town in Idaho," I said. "Not this," Maria said when we came on Santa Maria de Los Arcos, the town's enormous Romanesque and Gothic church. We passed it several times before entering for the afternoon pilgrims' mass. A dozen old Spanish widows in black joined two dozen of us pilgrims—scrubbed, tanned strangers.

The priest shone with love for his little congregation and for the pilgrims he welcomed, a few at a time, day after day. We were washed and unwashed, Catholic and not, and he knew it. I told Maria I was going to take Communion. "Me too," she whispered.

After mass he invited pilgrims back to the altar rail and he blessed us one by one in more languages than I could keep track of. "*Frances?*" he asked when he came to me. "English," I said. He prayed.

> *Lord, you called your servant Abraham out of Ur in Chaldea and watched over him during his wanderings: We ask that you watch over your servant, who, for love of your name, makes pilgrimage to Santiago de Compostela. Under your guidance, may he may reach the end of his journey safe and unhurt, strengthened with gratitude and filled with happiness, to rejoin those of his home. Through Jesus Christ our Lord. Amen.*

· · · · ·

Apostle James, pray for us. Holy Virgin, pray for us.

Maria was next. She said "*Ingles, por favor,*" before he asked. After he blessed us all, he promised he and his congregation would pray for us daily, and asked that we pray for the parish of Santa Maria de los Arcos at Saint James' tomb. After the service he took us to the choir loft to see the carved, polychromed *peregrinos*. He was like a boy sharing toys with playmates and introducing new friends to old friends. **D**

Room at the Inn?

· · · · ·

AFTER THE SERVICE Dad called Mom in California and then had me call for reservations at the Parador San Marcos in Leon. *Paradors* are state-run luxury hotels in historic buildings. They were too expensive for my budget, but Dad didn't want to pass up the opportunity to stay in the Royal Hospital de Peregrinos. "Dad's treat," he said before I called. The concierge asked only for my name. I hung up imagining I had accidentally called the San Marcos motor inn. Dad told me not to worry about it.

Heading back for a nap we saw two pilgrims I recognized from the *refugio* in Arre, packs on and maps out. I called out to them in Spanish, "*Por acá!* The *refugio's* the other way!" "No, no," one replied. We approached. Thinking they misunderstood me, I began directions in both Spanish and English. "No, no," she repeated, retreating slightly. She looked at her companion and then at me and said under her breath in English, "We are … going to a hotel." In her face I saw that she wanted a night of quiet rest and a long soak in a hot bathtub. I smiled. "Of course," I said, "I think there are some down that street."

We walked down the narrow stone lane toward the *refugio*. A screeching, followed by an

· · · · ·

abrupt honking, interrupted us. We jumped out of the car's way. It swerved around us up to the *refugio*'s gravel front yard and nearly blocked the gate. What kind of person would risk pilgrims' lives to get to a *refugio*? Walking around the car into the fenced yard we saw in the driver's seat, fussing at his collar, the German priest from Arre.

He pushed himself out of the car and began demanding to see the person in charge. The *hospitalero* came out of the *refugio* and told the priest what he already knew: the beds inside were for people who carry their own gear—foot pilgrims first, then those on horseback, then cyclists. He could offer the priest and his group the storage shed to sleep in. The priest demanded a place to hold his teaching sessions. "How will they ever learn about the Camino?!" "The storage shed," the *hospitalero* replied. Then he pointed to the car blocking the gate. "Oh, and you will have to move that."

The priest muttered to himself in German but moved the car. I sat on the *refugio*'s porch next to Lorenzo, a round Spaniard who had come on the pilgrimage to lose weight. He had arrived early at the *refugio* with a bottle of wine to welcome each pilgrim with congratulations and drink. The priest's charges arrived. We watched him ordering them to unload the gear from the car.

"They are where they should be," Lorenzo said as the last of the group entered the shed. "I carry my own bag and yet in Arre I slept on the floor, while they slept in beds." I agreed with Lorenzo, though I felt sorry for these kids. Certainly this was not the month in Spain they had pictured. I wondered if the priest, whom we never saw walking, yelled instructions at his marching troops from the car.

Later I hung out my wash with a young man wearing the group's bandana. He smiled and asked me if I carried my own pack. When I answered yes, he looked at me and said earnestly, "I wish I was doing that." I smiled sympathetically as the priest yelled to him that it was time for more Camino "lessons." *M*

· · · · · ·

Viana

· · · · ·

IN THE PLEASANTLY WARM afternoon, we left the trail to rest in a field of tall grass and yellow wildflowers. I spread my rain poncho in the shade of a poplar row and we sat to eat. A pilgrim stranger called out to us, "What a beautiful picture you two are!" I smiled and watched him walk on. We listened quietly to the birds above.

I was peeling an orange and letting the sticky juice run down my arms when Nick appeared. Staggering though the grass, he lurched toward us dumping his bag on the wildflowers. The pack hit the ground with a solid thud. "I'd keep walking but my knee is kind of bothering me," he said. "I should be able make Logroño tonight."

I asked about his pack.

"Its only forty pounds, I've carried lots heavier through the Yukon."

I suggested sending some extras back home. "Nah, my blisters are gone. The old guy's green stuff really worked."

He looked out and began musing on the ease of the Camino compared to his longer, nobler backpacking treks. I suggested a knee brace. He protested that he had been walking just fine that morning with a pair of Australians who averaged sixty kilometers a day. "I'd still be walking with them if it wasn't for this damn knee."

Worried that he would seriously hurt himself, I invited him to walk with us, offering to help him find a doctor in Viana. "Oh, my Spanish is really good. I could do that myself," he replied, "But I'll go with you to Viana anyway."

After another hour on the Camino we arrived in Viana, an elegant medieval town. Steel gates and familiar horn-height gouges in the stone walls told us we had just missed the town's own running of the bulls. We found the *refugio* inside a converted monastery. "I guess I'll stay here with you," Nick said at the door.

· · · · ·

Handsome wooden blinds kept the sleeping rooms dark and cool for napping. We picked beds. I watched Nick unpack. He took out a full size PLUS 30% FREE! bottle of shampoo. "I guess you use a lot of shampoo," I said. "No, not really," he replied, running a hand through his short blond hair and looking confused at the question.

Dad and Nick headed off to the showers. As I lay down to nap, a German walked in. From his large leg muscles pushing through his tight spandex shorts and his bow-legged walk I knew he was a cyclist. In the shadow behind him I saw a willowy woman in matching spandex.

"We all sleep together?" he exclaimed with horror in heavily accented English.

"Yes," I said calmly, assuming it was his first day in a *refugio*. They disappeared. I closed my eyes.

He returned shortly and tapped me on the shoulder. "There is a room over there," he said, pointing to the adjoining dorm. He knelt over me as if speaking to a child. "It is empty." He glanced at my bag, smiled, and then tossed his head in the direction of the door.

"I am fine here," I replied and closed my eyes again, wishing he would go away.

"But in the other room you will have more privacy!" he said, his voice no longer a whisper.

I sat up confused. There were plenty of available beds in our room if he wanted them. Or he could take the privacy of the empty room. His determination to claim territory angered me. I looked him in the eye and repeated, "I am fine here." The woman stood behind him looking silently at the floor. "Fine," he snapped as he turned and shepherded her into the empty room. Abruptly he returned and whispered, "You'll have more privacy this way. I like to make a lady happy."

When Dad returned from the shower, I told him of the interchange, still unsure why the German wanted me to move. "That cyclist creep? The guy was strutting around the co-ed bathroom naked," Dad said loudly, taking an aikido stance. "He can't talk to my daughter that way."

"Leave it alone, Dad." The German would sleep in the other room. There was nothing more to say. *M*

Bugs
· · · · ·

FROM VIANA we started our day in the dark. It would be a short walk, three hours into the city of Logroño. From there we would take the bus to Leon. Cutting out part of the Camino was disappointing but necessary; three and a half weeks wasn't enough time for us to make it to Santiago. Logroño began the flat arid plains between us and the Galician mountains. Skipping this section meant missing two hundred miles of wheat fields.

We walked alongside a river. It smelled stagnant and of sulfur. The breaking dawn revealed its ugliness. The shallow water barely moved through the sludgy riverbed. Newspapers and empty soda bottles littered the banks. We were alone on the trail except for the mosquitoes. The tiny black bugs darted around us as we passed. From behind, Dad looked like the pied piper, leading a dedicated and persistent flock.

Whimsy disappeared as the bugs began to bite. The more we walked the worse they got, clearly preferring me to Dad. "Because you're so sweet," Dad smiled. I wasn't amused.

I looked at the black freckles that covered my arms. There were too many to kill. As I swept my hands down my legs clearing them from one part of my body, they attacked another. My sweeping, bending, and beating before each step made me walk like a crazy pilgrim *penitente*. I wanted to sit down and cry, but that wouldn't keep the bugs from eating at me.

Finally the path turned away from the river and entered a pine forest. Dad walked in front

· · · · ·

of me, as the path was too narrow to walk side by side. The bites had not yet begun to itch, and I was relieved to walk normally again. Feeling better made me impatient, so I told Dad I wanted to walk out in front. "If you want," he said, smiling as he let me pass. A sticky thread dragged across my face as I stepped in front of him. Spider webs. "Well you were the one who wanted to walk in front," Dad said smugly.

We passed a graveyard. The thought of so many dead people made my bites itch. I wanted to talk to keep my mind on something else. I made a joke about Justin, my failed love. Dad winced. Not sure if he was angry or sympathetic, I left it alone.

We started to enter the Spanish *suburbos*—not "suburbs" but less than urban—neighborhoods of those too poor to live within the city's limits. The Camino ran behind the buildings. Attack dogs chained to the back of each house barked as we passed.

We neared an old woman sitting behind her house in a rusty lawn chair shaded by tin sheet and tarps. She was the first person we'd seen that day. She wore a plain cotton dress, comfortably tight, giving figure to her round body. "You need stamps!" she called out as we approached. On a table she had a pitcher of lemonade, a few glasses, a stamp, stamp pad, and a dish marked DONATIONS. She looked over our *credencias* and stamped them. Her unsteady hand and the shaky table made a double print on my *credencia*. Her stamp read "Felisa: *higos, agua y amor*,"—figs, water and love.

We were entering the city at rush hour. Suits, polished shoes, and vacant stares protected the morning commuters as they walked their familiar path through the wide streets and polluted air. They could afford to still be asleep. We could not. Even carrying our packs, we passed them as we walked.

Looking for the bus station we met a Brazilian who was catching a bus from Logroño back to France to fly home. He planned to resume his pilgrimage from here next summer. Happy to look for the bus station together, we found it within minutes. *M*

· · · · · ·

Buses to Leon

· · · · · ·

WE STRODE INTO the Logroño bus terminal at 8:28 a.m. and checked the schedule. The morning bus to Leon was going to leave in two minutes. Anxious as refugees, we entrusted our packs to the driver who stowed them in the luggage compartment beneath the bus.

As we clambered up into the bus's refrigerated air, I felt the weight of eight days' walking. We settled into plush reclining seats. I needed this break. No, I felt sick. I sneezed and hacked. Was it the cold smoky air? No, my intestines were uneasy too. The flu?

The bus pulled out. As we rode, all sorts of hip- and backaches came and went. I didn't want to say anything to Maria. Complaining to her about my discomfort had become a habit. I closed my eyes and imagined myself coughing in a lonely hotel room while Maria continued on without me. I saw myself alone, getting sicker, unable to call a doctor without Maria's fluent Spanish, and helpless to explain my symptoms if I managed to get medical help.

But if I stopped walking, my blisters would heal. My blisters frightened me. I checked them daily for infection and wondered whether the next day would finally be the day I couldn't walk. "The blisters," I reasoned, "aren't me; they're my own flesh turned against me, like a cancer." I worked to push aside paranoid thinking, and "simple logic" that took me inevitably from fear of infection to gangrene.

I opened my eyes. Maria was staring out at the Camino, a hundred meters from the road, to see if she recognized any pilgrims. Recognizing people would take some doing. I suggested we look for the Frenchman with his black dog. We didn't see him, but Maria spotted Olivier leading ahead with his power walk, and Sebastian ambling along behind.

Traveling without constantly watching for footing and environment felt odd. I sensed in my body how the pilgrims we passed were watching their step, paying attention to terrain

· · · · · ·

while keeping an eye ahead for yellow arrows. Gradually I relaxed enough to accept that the bus driver could guide the bus without me, and I slept. Maria woke me as we pulled into Burgos two hours later.

Two years before, our whole family with Rick, the children's godfather, had seen the Burgos Cathedral and what is probably the most beautiful urban section of the Camino, the elegant promenade along the river Arlanzón.

Today, for Maria and me Burgos was the bus depot, heavy diesel fumes, more cigarette smoke and fierce heat. We only glimpsed the cathedral. Maria said she was glad we were not trekking through. I stopped my impulse to argue with her and agreed. She was, after all, right; and as much as I resented needing her help, she was, in fact, treating me with great kindness.

We got our tickets for the 10:45 bus to Leon with just enough time to unload our packs, use the rest rooms in the terminal, get out the pilgrim guidebook, and re-load the packs on the next bus. Grumpy and self-pitying as I was, I could agree that our connections seemed incredibly lucky.

We read our pilgrim guide on this bus, and looked at our altitude map. When we arrived in Leon we would be at 800 meters. After resting there for a day and two nights' rest, we would begin a long, slow climb to 1,500 meters. Maria suggested we could hope for cooling as we climbed. And then from there cooler, more coastal weather in the remaining days to Santiago. I admitted such an improvement might be possible, but enjoyed warning her that we shouldn't count on it. Maria laughed at me, and managed to do it gently enough that she made me laugh a little too. **D**

. . . . . .

WHEN OUR BUS ARRIVED at Leon both of us were tired and hungry. Our map showed the *refugio* 3.5 kilometers from the bus station, an easy walk.

"This way," I said impatiently.

"No," Maria said gently, "this way," and she showed me where I'd misread the map. Bad enough that I had a runny nose, a cough, and sore feet. I had to be wrong too.

We crossed the river by San Marcos, the *parador* where we had reservations the following night. I mused about seeing if we could check in for two nights. Maria just kept on to San Isidoro, the fortress-church and monastery where the guidebook said we would find the *refugio*. I barely managed to keep up with her. At San Isidoro, a workman said the *refugio* had been relocated to a nearby convent. "Maria, it's supposed to be here."

"Come on, Dad," she said, "it's only a little further, and we'll find it soon enough."

I coughed several times, hobbling after her, suffering, I told myself, more than she knew. She stopped to ask someone directions. He pointed us back toward a plaza we'd just passed.

"Get him to show us!" I waved the map at her.

"We're doing fine," she replied.

"*You're* doing fine," I shot back.

"He agreed about our general direction."

I should trust this. Maria is a pathfinder. At age four her memory of landmarks and sense of direction guided Ellen through a new-to-us San Francisco. But I was feeling sick and sorry for myself. And my feet hurt.

"I'll wait on this bench while you find it," I said.

"We can rest when we get there, Dad. I'm tired too. Your blood sugar is low and you're not making any sense."

· · · · · ·

"I'm trying to conserve energy."

"Dad. Keep walking."

We found the *refugio* in a few blocks. Through a big doorway, two old nuns and the volunteer *hospitalera* welcomed us in. They offered lemonade and chairs in the shade. As we drank, the *hospitalera* explained to four boys that they could not stay a second night. If they needed more rest, she told them, perhaps the other *refugio* would take them. If not, they could stay in a *hostal*. "We offer one night's rest to pilgrims who have walked here."

It was our turn. The *hospitalera* glanced at our *credencias*, "Viana last night?" she said accusingly. "You didn't walk here."

"We are pilgrims," María insisted, "and we have already walked from Roncesvalles to Logroño. Only today we took the bus from Logroño."

"But today … ," she began.

"Today," I insisted, "we walked from Viana to Logroño and from the bus station here. Twelve kilometers. It's a short day but we need rest badly. We are staying two nights in Leon. Here tonight, and somewhere else tomorrow night."

"All right," she smiled, "here tonight. We can suggest a cheap *hostal* for tomorrow. Since you will have some time in Leon, you should stop to see San Marcos, the *parador* where the pilgrims stayed in the Middle Ages."

I thanked her for the suggestion and kept quiet about the next day's reservation.

We and thirty other pilgrims had mattresses on the floor in a convent schoolroom. The bathroom mirrors were at little-girl height. I could see myself from belt to chest. We washed up, and Maria found us a nice tavern where we ordered sautéed artichoke hearts, *chiperones* (stuffed squid cooked in its own ink), melon and beer.

We savored our lunch and rest. Maria got the check and took out her little account book, entering the lunch to our shared expenses. "Two thousand pesetas," she said. "The beers are my treat." She assured me I'd be fine in thirty-six hours. Good food and the prospect of a whole day's rest made me hope she might be right. **D**

Time Off
· · · · · ·

WE LEFT the *refugio* at 9 a.m. just as it closed for the morning. It was too early to check into San Marcos. We decided to go there anyway and ask the front desk to hold our bags until the afternoon. We followed the brass pilgrim shells embedded in the sidewalk to mark the Camino through Leon. They led us to San Marcos' sixteenth-century plateresque façade, the ornate stone relief carvings covering the length of Ferdinand and Isabella's pilgrims' hospital.

The lobby was huge, the mouth of a grand building, its ceilings fifty feet high. The adjacent two-story cloister flooded the lobby with natural light. Ahead of us a broad staircase led to the guestrooms. Wearing a sort-of clean shirt, ratty bandana, and dusty boots, I felt ashamed in so much grandeur. I feigned exhaustion and asked Dad, "Could you deal with this?"

"Getting tired of taking care of the old man?" he smiled and walked up to the concierge desk and began to explain our request in his best cut-and-paste Spanish. The concierge spoke slowly and deliberately, repeating Dad's words with improved grammar and vocabulary. "*Peregrinos*," he smiled pointing to our packs, "of course."

Reassured by his gentleness, I interrupted Dad, explaining our request more fluidly.

"If you want to leave your bags you may, but please," he protested, "I can check you in now!" He motioned to the bellhop to take our bags.

"We can carry them ourselves," I insisted, "We are used to carrying them." The bellhop

· · · · · ·

looked puzzled. He was just trying to do his job. I relinquished my pack to him. He took both bags by their straps and carried them like suitcases. I bit my lips to keep from giggling. He led us to our room, which was huge, and filled with such unfamiliar objects as pillows, sheets, and curtains. I took a long hot bath.

After a morning nap I wanted to see Leon's Gothic cathedral.

"I don't like Gothic," Dad protested.

"It's supposed to be the best stained glass in Europe."

"Right. If I liked stained glass I might like Gothic. But I'll go, as long as we can see San Isidoro." While we walked, Dad offered a mini-lecture on why he preferred Romanesque to Gothic.

It was Saturday. Outside the cathedral a wedding party posed for photos. We walked in. Another wedding was in progress. "Look what the sunlight is doing," Dad said. Reds, golds and oranges swirled in the vast space and on the warm stone. "Thank you, Maria. This feels alive. It's beautiful."

We went to Dad's Romanesque basilica of San Isidoro. Our tour guide seemed bored with the twelfth-century frescoes and annoyed with our questions. A woman behind us encouraged questions from her group of three. Dad slipped in with them. "Over here, Maria," he whispered, "she's a better guide." Marveling at a Mozarabic Bible, she smiled, "How I miss working here." I looked at the others in our group and realized these were her friends. We had crashed a private tour. I apologized and tried to move back to the other group. "No, no. You stay with us," she insisted. As we left we thanked her. "It is a joy to find someone else who loves Romanesque art," she said.

After the church we headed to the post office to post our extras home. Dad mailed five pounds, including a hardback book; I mailed two. We split the cost accordingly. We went to a pharmacy to get some bug cream for my bites. After looking unsuccessfully for a

Laundromat we decided to pay for the hotel's laundry service. Late that afternoon room service delivered neat stacks of perfectly pressed socks, T-shirts and underwear to our door.

Dad finished our day with his final gift to me, a dinner at the hotel's elegant restaurant. I dressed up in my good clothes, a wraparound skirt I carried for church services, a freshly pressed T-shirt and flip-flops. This time I felt no shame. The waiter seemed pleased when we asked for the chef's menu. "You order well," he said. *M*

Voices Outside
. . . . .

WE REACHED VILLAR DE MAZARIFE after a long, hot day on the plain. Villar's *refugio* was a locked, abandoned-looking house on the edge of town. As we read the note tacked to the door that said who to rouse for the key, Luciano, a young Brazilian pilgrim, arrived with it in hand.

The door opened into an airy passage that led through the house to a patio. Two rooms and a kitchenette opened off the passage. The patio seemed a cool, inviting ruin. Chickens pecked for bugs by a broken fountain. Flowering vines sagged from the wood pillars of the two-story portal that surrounded three sides, joining the back of the house, one patio wall, and the front of a barn. Plaster was missing from large sections of the fourth adobe wall, and breaks and cracks had been roughly patched with stone or brick.

The house lacked electricity. The toilet tank had to be filled with a bucket from the "shower," an outdoor shower head connected to the hose. We showered in our underwear, changed, and finished washing shorts and T-shirts. Maria scouted the kitchen and found a propane stove, a sink with running water, and a bag of rice. I was interested in the building and measured the patio for its proportions. I investigated the upstairs rooms and went to

. . . . .

have a look in the barn. A fierce dog chained inside growled and bared his teeth at me.

Maria suggested we look for a grocery. The streets were deserted. A small museum of Romanesque antiquities was closed, though posted hours claimed otherwise. We found the village's people gathered at the bar. Inside was hot, loud, and jammed with the older generation shouting and exclaiming over card games and dominoes. We ordered pre-made sandwiches and beer and took them outside, where the younger people sat at shady tables. At the table next to us, a group of local boys catcalled to girls who seemed annoyed but came to sit with them anyway.

Maria was eavesdropping and told me in English that they were talking about her, "the blonde pilgrim."

"Let's go," I said. On the way back we found the grocery, but it was closed. "It's OK, Dad," Maria said. "With our ham, prunes, nuts, and the rice back at the *refugio*, we could make a simple dinner."

No other pilgrims arrived. After dinner we said goodnight to Luciano, I barred the main door from inside, and we turned in.

Much later boisterous male voices below our window wakened me. They argued, and there was a drunken scuffle and taunting. I understood "blonde pilgrim," and not much else, but when I heard the door shake, I grabbed my stick and went downstairs.

The voices were loud on the other side of the door. When they tried it again, I saw it shake, but it held, solidly barred. Luciano slept soundly in one of the rooms off the passage. I climbed quietly back upstairs and lay down with my stick beside me. Maria slept. I got up again and lay her stick by her side and listened for a while. At last a neighbor awakened and scolded them, threatening to call their mothers if they didn't go home. They started singing and wandered off, and it was quiet. I lay back down.

The barn faced out to open farmland. Would they know a way in through the barn?

Would the dog keep them out? I got up again and investigated the upper floor of the portal that ran between the house and the barn's loft. The floor had holes in it and appeared too fragile to stand on. Anyone coming through the barn would have to cross an impassible walkway or face the dog. I slept.

In the morning Maria woke first and noticed I had moved our sticks. I told her of the voices outside and said, "Maria, I am glad you are not walking this alone."

"If I were walking alone I wouldn't have stayed in such an empty place," she said, "and if there had been trouble I could have gotten help from Luciano." **D**

Fighting
· · · · ·

WE ENTERED PUENTE DE ÓRBIGO defeated, cutting our planned day short as Dad's blisters pained his feet and my patience. We crossed the long, chariot-wide Roman bridge to Hospital de Órbigo. On this bridge Suero de Quiñones, a fourteenth-century knight, made his famous challenge to unhorse any pilgrim knight who tried to pass without conceding Quiñones' lady the fairest. Children bathed in the broad Río Órbigo beneath us.

We found the *refugio* not far from the bridge, a newly restored medieval pilgrims' hostel on a patio around a stone well covered with tiny white flowers. "If anyone cared, Villar could look like this," Dad said.

The *hospitalero*, a friendly German my father's age, led us into the small office. While he stamped our *credencias*, I counted out enough change for us both and put it in a small locked box as he directed. We left to choose beds.

The *hospitalero* found us. Holding out the change in his hand, he explained that our pay-

· · · · ·

ment fell four hundred pesetas short. Perhaps I had mistaken the similar 500 and 100 peseta coins.

Mistaking coins was common enough among tourists, but I knew Spain, I had lived in Spain. I had Spanish friends. "Impossible," I snapped, certain I had paid the correct amount. The mistake had to have been his.

The *hospitalero* held out the coins for my inspection. He noted that I had paid into a locked box. We were the only pilgrims yet to pay, so ours was the only money in the box. He insisted I was wrong. Dad said nothing. I took out my change purse and showed there was no 500 peseta coin. Where was the 500 peseta piece that I had that morning? The *hospitalero* relented, but I persisted. I wanted him to say I was right. Dad, realizing we argued over three dollars, suggested that we give a 400 peseta "donation" to the beautiful *refugio*. I reluctantly agreed to this semantic compromise.

We retreated from the *refugio* back toward a bar beside Quiñones' bridge. Under the heavy gray sky, I couldn't free myself from a feeling of injustice. "I hope he feels stupid when he finds our money," I thought to myself. A large drop of rain fell squarely on my head.

Snug in the deserted bar, we watched picnickers fleeing the downpour and settled in with our journals to write. My writing was angry. How could I have forgotten that *hospitaleros* were volunteers? That the German worked long hours for no money? That, like all other *hospitaleros*, he had walked the pilgrimage himself?

Dad's head kept popping up and looking at something behind me. I turned. On the TV above the bar Jackie Chan punched and kicked his way through a climactic fight scene. I looked at Dad, shocked that a dubbed action film would keep his attention. Dad's favorite movies are slow, intellectual queries into thought and emotion. If they're foreign, all the better. And yet here he sat entranced, pointing and laughing, the happy Buddha, as Jackie kicked, fought, flipped and fell.

. . . . . .

The credits ran with a series of outtakes, mostly Jackie laughing at stunt-gone-wrong mishaps. In the worst, we watched Jackie break his ankle jumping on to a moving train. We saw him helicoptered out to a hospital and then returning to film more stunts, his cast painted to look like a shoe. Jackie smiled as he pulled up his pant leg to reveal his trickery to the camera.

"Compared to this, our pilgrimage is nothing!" Dad laughed. *M*

Passion
. . . . .

IN MODERN SPAIN, Maria told me, parents of unmarried couples were particular about keeping old-fashioned appearances, including the couples not traveling together. But apparently they judged the pilgrimage a chaste-seeming way for young couples to spend time together, at least many young Spanish couples walked the pilgrimage together. I had read that medieval couples were sometimes sent on the pilgrimage with vows to remain chaste until they could return from Santiago to be married. Perhaps some of that tradition lingered in people's thinking.

Maria also guessed parents thought that any couple who could successfully spend a month walking and working together, seeing each other tired, dusty and disheveled, would make a happy marriage. She had been noticing which couples were kind and patient with each other and invited me to observe with her. In the *refugios* couples slept in adjacent bunks like brother and sister.

Tired, tender good-nights and chaste kisses barely whispered the passion they must, I thought, dream in their sleep. I guessed at this from my own dreams of Ellen so far away.

In Órbigo Maria spotted a young couple who seemed oddly clingy. They had just begun walking; it would be their first night in a *refugio*. As people turned in, the girl whispered

. . . . .

something to her boyfriend about being afraid of the dark. They bunked across the aisle from me, above and below.

I woke a few hours later. The room was as dark as a cave. The steady breathing rhythms of a dozen sleepers made a peaceful music in the dark. Across the aisle I heard his whisper and her reply. I heard him climb down to her. I tried to go back to sleep, ignoring the creaking springs and the hushed urgency of their breathing.

They left before anyone else the next morning. Later that day we passed them. She seemed hurt. He reproached her for it.

"Not enough kindness," Maria said, "They won't make it."

"To Santiago?" I asked.

"Not to Santiago. And not together." **D**

Santa Catalina *sin Plantillas*

· · · · · ·

AGAIN AT SANTA CATALINA, the *refugio* was locked. Here the note said the key was at "the other bar." So Santa Catalina with its old stone houses in such good repair was not only prettier than Villar, it was bigger, a two-bar town. Maria offered to get the key. I thanked her. It was very hot, and my feet hurt.

In the shade of an outdoor milling shed by the *refugio*, I took off my boots and slipped on my sandals. I studied my feet. The dull ache I'd felt for the last few kilometers was a new blister. I walked over to the tap and poured handfuls of water over my head. At least I could do something about the heat.

Two French women arrived and greeted me. I was pleased I could be unselfconscious with my rusty French. Talking with fellow pilgrims felt good, whether it meant stumbling

· · · · · ·

in Spanish, struggling with others' limited English, or chattering in my high-school French.

These women were about my age. We'd seen them during the day. I told them Maria was my daughter. They said each year they left their husbands and children behind for a two-week walking tour. They explained, with some laughter, that their families thought their walking pleasure absurd, but were glad the two had each other for companions.

When Maria returned with the key, the women had taken off their boots and were removing their insole liners to dry in the sun.

"You should try that, Dad," Maria suggested. "Maybe getting them really dry will help with your blisters."

Did my boots have such removable liners? I reached in and easily removed my paper-thin, flattened liners. "My God, they're completely worn out!" Maria exclaimed.

"Behold, the cause of your blisters," one French woman said. "You should replace them." Her theory and suggestion seemed quite plausible. Lacking cushioning between my feet and the hard structure of the boot, my soles would take a beating. It was also evident there would be nowhere in Santa Catalina to buy insoles.

Maria and I went to the nearer bar to get some cider and sit in the shade. The sun sank low and a little breeze came up. The paving stones of the street began to cool off. We sat on a stone step across from the bar, watching a handful of old people from the village walk toward us. They were in heated argument with Pablo, an old man with a red vascular bulge on his face that was as big as a second nose. One of the widows accused Pablo of listening to no one and called him arrogant. He looked contrite until she said something more that made him angry enough to shout back. She shouted all the louder. They argued their way past us and continued up the empty street until they were a row of shadows like cut-outs figures against the sun. And then, still arguing, they turned the corner out of sight.

I asked the bartender where we could get something to eat. "*No hay tienda aquí,*" he said in Spanish, and then in English, "I will cook spaghetti for you." Then back to Spanish, "If other pilgrims want to eat, tell them to let me know. Eight o'clock." We went back to lie down in the *refugio*. The air was fresh and hinted at cooling.

The French women joined us for dinner and I worked to translate their French for Maria, except when the bartender joined in with Spanish and English, and then I was translating his English into French. He had this bar and a T-shirt shop his son ran in Los Angeles. "*Plantillas*," the bartender explained, was the Spanish word for the insoles I needed to replace. **D**

It Stings
· · · · · ·

WE APPROACHED RABANAL, only six miles beyond Santa Catalina. The heat was intense. Maria was being patient with my pace. I had a nasty headache, and we hadn't even begun the afternoon. It didn't help to know I was injuring my feet for lack of good insoles. I kept rehearsing my conversation in the hiking store in San Francisco, regretting all the questions I didn't ask when I bought the socks and laces for the trip. I had good boots with plenty of wear still left in them. I felt smug that they were comfortably broken in. If only I had put them on the counter and asked the salesman, what do these need?

The last kilometer to Rabanal was steep. I felt the searing hot pavement through my boots. With the town in sight, words came from my mouth I hated to hear: "Can we stop?"

I knew Maria worried that we were losing momentum and wouldn't make Santiago, but she didn't complain. Her only hint of impatience was offering to walk ahead and check things out.

When I arrived, she was waiting with a couple of other pilgrims in a sliver of shade
· · · · · ·

against the *refugio*'s gate. When the gate opened early, it felt like a mercy. We stepped into a cool, shadowy arch through the two-story building. The *refugio* shared a courtyard with the family's house and some working farm buildings. The pilgrims' dormitory and showers were new and spotlessly clean. As always, we paid only a couple of dollars for our beds. Isabel, who signed us in, appeared to be the center of a circle of family and friends who helped in the *refugio*.

I showered and sat in the shade, treating my blisters the only way I knew—puncturing them with needle and thread covered in antibiotic ointment and leaving the thread dangling from the blister to continue draining. Isabel saw me and said that she had learned a medical treatment that would cure my blisters. She promised it effective, though quite painful. I said I would try it.

She returned with Betadyne and a new hypodermic syringe sealed in its box. She probed my blisters gently with her fingers as she described the procedure and warned me again how much it would hurt. I didn't understand her explanation but nodded anyway. "Tomorrow you will be happy for this," she said.

She unwrapped the hypodermic, pierced the blister, drew out the faintly yellow fluid and squirted it on the ground. Where the blister had bulged, a whitish coin-sized circle of white skin sagged. I had only felt a little pressure when she punctured the callused skin.

"That didn't hurt at all," I said.

"The hurt comes next," she said, drawing Betadyne into the syringe. She pierced the skin again and slowly injected the purple-brown fluid into the blister, swelling it full again. Bulging with Betadyne, it was now the color of a very nasty bruise. I don't understand how this helps, I thought, but it doesn't hurt.

Suddenly the Betadyne touched some tiny sore inside the large blister. It felt like a hot needle probing the raw, tender wound. I gasped pushing down my urge to run or hit. The worst pain subsided. Betadyne trickled from the two holes in my blistered skin. A nasty stinging hung on.

"Shall we do the one with the thread?" Isabel asked.

'Yes, please," I whimpered.

As I took the thread out, she re-filled the needle with Betadyne. The same searing pain. I sat for a while and then put on clean socks and my sandals. My feet were sore, but I could walk. We went for lunch and groceries.

As I tried to sleep that night, my feet ached. I decided the treatment had failed and dreaded how much more it would hurt in the morning. **D**

High Places
. . . . .

WE LEFT RABANAL before dawn. It was cold and still. As usual it was painful putting my boots on, but now my feet were feeling good. Isabel's cure had worked. Without *plantillas*, I would get new blisters, but I had learned an effective way to deal with them.

Frequent switchbacks led us up the mountainside. I was grateful we hadn't attempted this climb in killing heat. With sunrise, a stinging wind came up. The mountains offered no shelter at all. We gave up our plan to eat breakfast by the path and pushed on to Foncebadón, a desolate village that had grown up around the monk Guacelmo's twelfth-century pilgrim hospital.

Stone houses in Foncebadón were boarded up. The church was doorless and partially unroofed. Inside we found the recent rubble and tools of a restoration in progress. It was even colder in the church, so we moved to a sheltered spot behind it to sit and eat, hoping the thin sunlight might warm us a little. I told Maria that working summers in a fruit cannery I'd

. . . . . .

learned that "warm mornings bring hot days; cold mornings begin warm days."

"Dad," Maria said shivering, "It's too cold to talk about warm places and too cold to sit still. Can we just eat and get going?" We finished our bread, cheese and juice in silence and set out again.

Half an hour later we saw Cruz De Ferro in the distance. The "Cross of Iron" is the highest point of the whole Camino, a landmark wooden pole as tall as a ship's mast rising from a cone of stones higher than a house. The two-foot-high wrought iron cross atop the pole looked tiny. Roncesvalles, Cruz de Ferro and O'Cebreiro (the next summit) were the highest points of the Camino. This was a true peak experience. An ongoing, altitude-exhilarated mountain party cheered us on from the top of the mound.

Guacelmo had placed his original iron cross atop such a pole to claim and transform this ancient Celtic mound of stones to a marker of the Christian's pilgrimage. Long before the Romans conquered Spain, travelers had been tossing votive stones to Celtic gods on this mound. Medieval and modern pilgrims carried on the gesture under the blessing of the cross. Some carried small stones from home. We hadn't thought to bring stones from California, but picked up two on the ridge of windmills in Navarra.

We scrambled up the mound to add our stones. Another pilgrim, headed back down, offered to take our photo with Maria's camera. We waved for the picture and shouted our greetings to fresh pilgrims arriving. Rocks flew as Maria slid down to retrieve her camera. I carried another pilgrim's camera down to take his picture.

Pilgrims arriving here, scrambling up to toss stones, and exchanging cameras and greetings, would continue all day; but we were too cold to linger. We followed the Camino along a ridge, down a bit, then up again toward Manjarín, the next abandoned village. **D**

· · · · ·

I FELT MISERABLE that morning. The constant uphill walking aggravated my knee, and the cold burned my bare legs and arms. Mostly I was angry with myself for mailing my sweater and overshirt back home. On the sun-baked plain of Leon this had seemed a brave embracing of a "less is more" philosophy. In the cold wind of Leon's mountains it felt like stupid optimism.

"Better cold than hot," Dad suggested in his long-sleeved overshirt.

"Easy for you to say," I snapped back.

"You can wear my shirt if you want," he offered. I declined, preferring to hold tight to my bad mood.

Coming down off the ridge from the Cruz de Ferro we came upon a compound of stone huts, sheltered from the wind and slightly off the road. We had heard of Manjarín; a pilgrim *refugio* was being built in the ruins of a town. The place looked deserted and uninhabitable. I heard a bell clanging loudly.

By the entrance of the *refugio* a pole with cartoon-like arrows listed distances to Santiago, Rome, Jerusalem, and Machu Pichu. A boom box blared scratchy Gregorian chant. "Come have some coffee," the *hospitalero* called, waving us in. "In" was a rough court with picnic tables sheltered by sheds and stone walls. The largest shed covered a small bookstore, with shells, souvenir pins, and old-fashioned water gourds. "Gifts from Manjarín," a woman said from behind the counter as she poured us two cups of coffee. It surprised me how good and hot the coffee was. Good Spaniards never serve bad coffee.

We sat on the bench with our boots off, washing our feet with our rubbing alcohol. The icy wind dried them quickly. Dad turned his feet to inspect the smaller dead blisters. Isabel's treatment was working. Dad asked the man if the cold was typical. "In summer, no," he replied, this weather was strange. The previous few days' heat had been unbearable.

I asked the *hospitalero* about the distance sign.

"Santiago is right, I just made up the other distances," he said.

I showed him my rain poncho that said Machu Pichu Hotel, a gift from my godfather. He laughed. "I wanted to put Mecca, but was afraid it would offend people. So I put Machu Pichu."

The woman added more coffee to my cup. Around her neck she wore a tiny silver pilgrim shell. "From my last pilgrimage," she told me. "You can get one in Santiago." I asked her what it was like to live and work in such an outpost. Worse in the winter, she said, for the cold.

"Pilgrims can miss the *refugio* in the snow, so we must keep a careful watch."

I looked out on the mountain and tried to imagine it abandoned and covered with snow. How lonely it would be to spend days, eyes on the horizon, without seeing a soul.

On the wall of the shed I recognized an old photo I'd seen in the restaurant in Órbigo— a man with a blank stare standing in a long black cloak and felt hat, in his hand a tall staff, around his neck a pilgrim shell. I couldn't make out the signature at the bottom of the photo.

Next to the photo hung a framed newspaper article, telling the story of Manjarín: How the regional power authority had threatened to cut off electricity to the area. How Tomás, the founder of this *refugio*, went on a hunger strike to bring media attention to his cause. How his action saved not only the *refugio*, but also the less visible mountain dwellers. I looked at the picture, I looked at the signature, and I looked at our host. All Tomás. Seeing more pilgrims approach, he jumped to ring the bell. *M*

· · · · · ·

Molinaseca
· · · · · ·

Maria was doing better after coffee. From Manjarín we followed the road. An arrow pointed us off the road and up over a ridge where we began the very steep descent to Acebo. Handsome signs along the path invited pilgrims to stop at La Taberna de José for "a really good lunch." Acebo suddenly appeared beneath us, slate-roofed, stone buildings cascading down a rocky hillside, looking more like Wales than Spain. We were entering Galicia, Celtic Spain.

At the road two bicycles shot past us, down into town. "They are going to get themselves killed," I said to Maria as we walked by a metal sculpture of a bicycle wheel, a memorial to a pilgrim who had skidded head-on into a car. We passed a bar that wasn't José's. Inside sat the cyclists. "I guess José only posted his signs on the footpath," Maria said. Toward the end of town, just as I began worrying we'd gone too far, another sign directed us to José's, one block over.

The warming day made it delightful to eat outside. It was a little early but José opened up for us. Other pilgrims filled the outdoor tables as he served us *sopa Gallega* (Galician tomato and chicken soup), *empanada* (a wonderfully delicate pastry filled with cheese), and a cinammony *arroz con leche* (Spanish rice pudding), all very fresh, hearty and delicious. Unlike the Scots and Irish, Spanish Celts eat well.

From Acebo to Molinaseca was down and down and down—great vistas, rolling clouds, and a beastly beating from the hard soles of my boots. By the bottom of the mountain it was hot, even though huge billowy white clouds sailed over us and we had only patches of sunshine.

I had new blisters but knew how to deal with them. Molinaseca would complete our longest day's walk so far on the Camino. We knew now we could break thirty kilometers

· · · · ·

(eighteen miles). I offered thanks out loud to Jesus for a grand day and to Isabel on the other side of the mountain for healing my feet.

We crossed a Romanesque footbridge over a dammed up swimming river full of children and lined with sunbathers. The water was intensely blue, and the sunbathers' grass park alongside it perfectly green. The town was traditional half-timbered with plastered wattle infill and a few Renaissance stone houses with crests above their doors.

The *refugio* was on the far side of town, a ruined old church recently rebuilt with a new steeply peaked roof and a massive central fireplace to warm sleeping lofts. Its immense central skylight captured all the sun's heat. It was an oven. At Maria's suggestion we claimed an empty overflow tent in the field behind.

We showered and did our wash. Hanging our laundry in the hot still air, we marveled at the difference between Molinaseca and the mountaintop. We went looking for *plantillas* for my boots. No luck there, but did get a hypodermic needle and Betadyne. The pharmacist assured us that we could get sturdy *plantillas* at Continente, a store in Ponferrada.

Back at the *refugio*, I tried administering Isabel's treatment to myself for the first time. The Betadyne's sting didn't surprise me this time. But I hadn't guessed how hard it would be to keep pushing the liquid through the hypodermic, much harder than just trying to hold still and bear the pain. Maria offered to do it for me. I said I thought I needed to do it myself. I was putting my socks back on when an old man walked up to me. He was probably seventy-five and dressed in slacks and a white shirt, like older people we'd seen strolling in town. He smiled broadly and said, "My daughter taught you that." Seeing my confusion, he added, "Isabel, in Rabanal."

"Ah yes," I smiled with him. "How did you get here?"

"Today," he said, "I walked from Rabanal, like you. My children will drive here to pick

· · · · · ·

me up. I'm too old to carry a pack, and my stiff old hip won't make the climb to O'Cebreiro. But I wanted to walk this. Maybe my last time on the Camino," he said, still smiling, and added, "for this year anyway." **D**

N o w h e r e
. . . . . .

FROM MOLINASECA we could see Ponferrada, a vast urban expanse separating us from our day's destination, Villafranca. Coal and iron had made Ponferrada rich, and I could smell both in the air. We looked down on the valley drowning in a ghost lake of smog. At least with so much city we were sure to find good insoles for Dad.

The Camino led us almost immediately into Ponferrada's old center, a tiny fraction of the city compared to the bloated modern section beyond it. The empty streets led us past a medieval castle built to protect pilgrims. It was closed. Stores would not open for another hour, so I suggested a leisurely breakfast. Our coffee, toast, and orange juice were good but gone too quickly. Killing time was hard; knowing the cause of Dad's problem, I was impatient to fix it.

The route through the city was poorly marked, as if the Camino were an unwelcome visitor. Beyond the old city streets turned ugly with 1970s industrialism. Four-lane throughways, the wet dreams of traffic engineers, replaced plazas and parks as we walked by unending blocks of cut-out concrete apartment buildings. When we asked for directions people hesitated. I couldn't tell if they were angry or frightened.

We stopped each time we saw a shoe store to see if they carried *plantillas*. With Dad's feet hurting, I would run off the marked route to ask at any place that looked promising. Store

. . . . . .

after store offered only flimsy cut-to-fit insoles and the assurance that Continente would have sturdier options. I was left to retrace my wasted steps to where Dad and the Camino waited for me.

Just as it seemed we might be leaving the city, a man directed us a few blocks over to Continente. With so many Spaniards convinced that it would have what we wanted, I had assumed we were heading to a sporting goods store. Standing in its shadow, it became clear that Continente was the Spanish cousin of K-Mart. A security guard made us leave our packs at the front desk.

We set to our task. It took some time to find the footwear aisle. There we found an extensive, carefully marked and beautifully displayed selection of flimsy cut-to-fit insoles. This type of insole could bunch and curl underfoot with hiking and make Dad's feet *worse*. We stood quietly staring at the display. The last major city before Santiago had failed us. "Come on, Maria," Dad said, "let's get out of here."

Finding our way back to the Camino we discovered that what had looked to be the end of Ponferrada was a large construction site followed by street after street of three- and four-story buildings. I was tired and I wanted out of this endless sprawl. Why wouldn't this damn city end? We kept walking, my eyes ever forward, looking for a bench or a small park. In other towns we could rest on a doorstep, trusting the hospitality of strangers inside. Here women sweeping their porches kept an eye on us as we passed, as if to say, "Move along." We ate our lunch on a concrete traffic separator.

We started walking again. Eventually vineyards replaced the buildings. Dad whispered, "Isn't it beautiful?" I grumbled. Grapes grew too low to offer any shade. The taste of Ponferrada's air lingered in my mouth. We kept walking through vineyards toward the mountains.

Our first of view of Villafranca began with two rows of houses built into the sides of a

· · · · · ·

shallow canyon. Gardens spilled over low fences into the wild below. Smoke from burning leaves hung motionless in the canyon. Knowing I was just a few minutes from putting down my bag I thought to myself, "Thank God, this day is over!" *M*

The Door of Mercy
· · · · ·

WE HAD DECIDED to rest up for O'Cebreiro with two nights and a whole day in Villafranca del Bierzo. From Leon pilgrims had talked of O'Cebreiro, some repeating what they'd heard of the village's startlingly beauty, others hoping the beginning of Galicia would mean cooler weather and great seafood. But the conversation always returned to the dreaded last five kilometers to O'Cebreiro, where the Camino was rumored to climb straight up.

To me "straight up" sounded like rock climbing, us stuck on a ledge below O'Cebreiro, searching for handholds on a rock face. Was the climb actually dangerous? One pilgrim claimed that a recent heart attack victim had to be carried some distance so a helicopter could reach him. I didn't believe this story, but it frightened me. Our guidebook said most pilgrims paid to have their packs motored up the road from Villafranca to O'Cebreiro; I wondered if we should hitch a ride up.

When we arrived in Villafranca we settled into an inexpensive seventeenth-century inn (with nineteenth-century plumbing added a long way down the hall). The place was incongruously named Hostal Commercial. Plain as it was, by pilgrim standards it seemed spacious, quiet, and luxurious. Next morning we enjoyed a late breakfast by the outdoor market—savory *empanada*, fresh orange juice and great coffee. Then we shopped for things small enough to carry, silver bracelets for the boys, a hair clip for Sasha, and a red-and-gold silk patchwork knapsack that would hold our lunch, water and first-aid/sewing kit for the

· · · · ·

packless day to O'Cebreiro. Of course we also scouted shoe and boot stores for *plantillas* but found none.

We went to mass for Saint James' Day in Villafranca's Romanesque pilgrim church. We were just a week's walk from Santiago. In the Middle Ages, sick and dying pilgrims who got this far, but feared they would die before Santiago, passed through this church's "Door of Mercy." By doing so they receive indulgences equal to completing the pilgrimage. I hoped they'd open the Door of Mercy at the dismissal so we all could pass through, but it stayed locked.

We jostled our way out the big doors at the back of the church into a crowd pressed hard against the building. I almost bumped into our Frenchman from Pamplona, who smiled his greeting and asked if we remembered him. He said his dog was at the *refugio*.

All at once everyone turned back toward the doors. The crowd parted at an ethereal jingling, like a hundred tiny bells, and Saint James emerged from the church walking almost above the crowd. Four men carried his statue on their shoulders. Their unison steps on the stairs and uneven hillside made the statue's cloth sleeve sway rhythmically from his upraised arm. The saint seemed to wave a blessing over us. I turned to speak to the Frenchman, but he was gone.

As the crowd dispersed, we walked next door to Refugio Ave Fenix to ask about having our packs ferried up. This phoenix was rising stone by stone from the ruins of the medieval pilgrims' hostel. The Fenix hauled pilgrims' packs to O'Cebreiro to raise funds for their restoration work. We wandered through rubble, dust and tools to admire the nearly completed common room. Through a stone arch we stepped directly into Fenix's plastic-tented bar, the gateway to a funky village of scrounged make-do tent quarters for stone workers and pilgrims.

The *hospitalero* said we should leave our packs overnight. We fetched them from the

Hostal Commercial, paid our 300 pesetas, and added them to the heap of packs in one corner of the tent. That was it—no claim check or receipt. Nothing. Would we find the bar at O'Cebreiro where they'd be left for us? What if someone else claimed them? What if ours got left by accident? Maria reasoned that if the *refugio* lost people's packs we'd have heard. She wasn't speaking to my worry exactly, but I heard. To climb this mountain we had to trust the Fenix and leave everything behind. **D**

On Wings of the Phoenix

WE STARTED OUR MORNING tiptoeing down Hostal Commercial's dark corridors by penlight, descending the long stairway, and letting ourselves out into the cold. With my overshirt packed and on its way to O'Cebreiro, we jogged to warm up. The highway shot dramatically through a tunnel and then began a lazy climb alongside a river.

After a few hours we made our way through neat rows of diesel trucks and buses, engines running, for a coffee break. The truck stop could have been in Colorado. I held the chrome door for two young women in skirts with staffs and backpacks.

"Pretty," I said.

"But they won't make it," Maria whispered, eyeing their heeled sandals. We savored good coffee with the Spanish truckers and moved on.

Ten minutes later we flew past the young women who seemed quite content to merely stroll through these pleasant green woods. I envisioned our strong pace rushing us along the beginning of our mapped route to the spot where the legendary climb of O'Cebreiro would finally begin, but this gentle climb stretched on and on. I figured each easy step now meant we'd find ourselves making a steeper climb at the end of the day.

Maria spotted a Camino marker that sent us up a sheer, narrow trail, and I charged it eagerly. But that path ended at a gouged mountainside, excavations, terracing, and criss-crossing tractor roads wildly decorated with yellow lines and arrows. Were they construction markers or a bad joke? Other confused pilgrims appeared behind us. Together we picked our way back down to the highway.

Where the road finally began to climb, the Camino cut to a far steeper country lane that twisted through farms and woods. Water gurgling out everywhere hinted that verdant Galicia began with this mountain. So far the stiff climb felt good, I thought, but it will get worse.

Around noon, as the road snaked up a rocky face, one strap of our knapsack gave way. We stopped in the shade of a vine-strangled evergreen to eat our lunch. Maria re-stitched the sack, commenting that we were finally using the sewing kit for sewing. Thus far we'd known needle and thread as blisters therapy.

Our way left the lane, swept down a small hollow and up through dense forest. Trees and switchbacks hid the sheer hillside until we emerged and looked back. Forest and valley far below us shimmered in bright heat. From here we climbed unsheltered—hot, thirsty mortals carrying nothing but our bodies into a realm of blazing light.

We finished the last of our bottled water and thirsted still. Our way dropped down a little and then climbed abruptly into a village that was not O'Cebreiro, an unknown village not on our map. There was no *tienda* where we could buy water, but we drank greedily from a spring marked "*Agua Potable*," and re-filled our water bottles. And I poured lots of water over my head.

Beyond the village our way leveled out and ran true a hundred feet below the ridge. Scattered pilgrims ahead of us grew smaller in the distance, until the bright haze swallowed them whole. I worried now that the climb straight up would be in this merciless sun. We walked another hour numbed by light and heat until we came on a walled garden right on the ridge. Walking beside the sun-baked wall was stifling until the wall ended. There a cool breeze appeared out of nowhere.

We had arrived without any kilometers straight up.

Our pilgrim village was cast Celtic silver on a green ridge. Houses, church, and a couple of tiny bars, poised in the sky. The town was just two cobbled streets wide, all silvery stone with shining slate roofs. To the west the mountain fell into Galicia just as steeply as the face we'd just traversed. I was shivering, chilled by my sweat in the cold wind, and stunned to imagine wintering here in blinding gales and snow.

"Dad, let's get something to eat," Maria said.

"Something hot," I agreed. "We can look for our packs later." Beside the pre-Romanesque church with its Scottish-looking squared-off tower was an elegant little inn. "Dad's treat," I said as we stepped into snug warmth. A huge fire in the corner reflected bronze on silvery stone walls.

"Would you like lunch?" the host asked us.

"*Sí! Por favor.*"

I saw my pack and then Maria's in a great stack behind the counter. Fenix had dropped them just where earth touched heaven. Salty with dried sweat, tired and dusty, we sat at a white-clothed table and feasted on hearty soup, oven-hot bread, red wine and sausage. **D**

. . . . . .

Seeing

. . . . .

IN O'CEBREIRO our room's four double bunks lined both walls like a ship's cabin. We arrived to find Julio and Veronica, a Spanish couple we'd met earlier, sitting on two of the upper bunks. Julio was carefully tending to Veronica's blister. Two more pilgrims came in and took beds. After dinner we turned out the lights. We didn't worry about the packs on the two empty beds below us.

I was sound asleep when the lights came back on. Bags rustled and hit the floor. Awakened but groggy I tried to ignore the middle-aged Spanish couple who were getting ready for bed. The woman left for the bathroom and the man propped the door open to yell something to her.

Julio sat up. "*Oye*, we're sleeping in here!" The man mumbled something. Julio threw himself back on the bed with a frustrated grunt. I was angry too. This man had broken the unwritten rules that allowed a hundred tired pilgrims to sleep together peaceably. After more talking and rustling of packs the lights finally went out.

We awoke at 6 a.m. Our roommates still slept. The *refugio* was dead silent. Coming back from brushing my teeth I passed the hall window. The laundry line I'd seen last night was gone. The green framed window square looked like a modernist painting, *Study in Gray #7.* Damn. Fog.

I went back to the room. I knew Dad wanted to get an early start, but our first section of Camino ran beside the road. In this fog cars wouldn't see us. An extra hour of sleep was our wisest choice. There were already plenty of shrines to pilgrims killed by cars. At 7:30 the fog had swallowed up our mountaintop, and we could have been in Sam Spade's San Francisco. We went for coffee at the nearest bar.

As we entered the old stone building the fierce wind slammed the door behind us. The

. . . . . .

bar was cozy with wooden floors and rustic wooden furniture. A blazing fire in the fireplace warmed the room. The bartender apologized that the coffee machine was broken, but said he would do his best. As the place filled with pilgrims, he made drip coffee two cups at a time. We felt grateful.

When we finally left O'Cebreiro, the fog still hung thick. Now everything was dull white. Objects emerged from the fog only as gray shadows, color only evident in the few feet ahead of us. Engine noise was the only warning of road danger, and the fog distorted the sound unpredictably. A truck roared behind us but never appeared. A car swept by us without a sound. Cyclists, crazy with the downhill, flew silently past, oblivious to danger. When the wind didn't blow on us, there was eerie quiet.

The wind kicked up as we passed a large steel statue of Saint James, his hat pulled low, his cloak flapping behind him as he leaned against a fierce wind. "He must look very strange in good weather," I said to Dad, holding my own hat to keep it from flapping in the wind.

The Camino left the roadway for a very, very slick stony path. Where it wasn't stone, there was a thin layer of mud on hardened earth. Dad fell. We agreed to slow our pace.

We stopped in another bar for a snack and more coffee. The bar and *refugio* sat at a cross-roads. There were no other buildings in sight. The place was packed with pilgrims talking loudly. They welcomed us in and made yet more space for a family who arrived with their cold, tired little girl.

The couple who had been so loud in our room the night before walked in. The man saw the little girl and crouched down to make her a pilgrim's cross of string and twigs at the end of her staff. She proudly showed it to her parents. His act of kindness annoyed me. But why? Did I want the bad guys to stay bad? Dad whispered to me, "I guess you never can tell about people."

One man about my age sat by the window staring at the fog, pain on his face. He told me the long climb the day before was just too much. I could hear his doubt in the words "too much." He thought he wouldn't make it to Santiago. I tried to offer him words of comfort. We had passed the last peak. The rest of the climb would be downhill or flat. He shook his head. I tried to show him our altitude map, but he wouldn't look. He was determined to stay. Having let go of the fear that we'd never make it, it was hard to leave him there, still staring out into the fog.

We walked down off the mountain, out of the fog, down hillsides with long sunny vistas, down stony green paths and fields of blue wildflowers. I thought of the man. Tomorrow he will walk through this. And he will know, he'll be all right. *M*

Pilgrims' Mass
· · · · ·

THE PILGRIMS' MASSES we attended had disappointed me. I thought a liturgy to end a day of walking and quiet reflection should teach us something new about common prayer. At O'Cebreiro the priest's posted invitation had looked promising, but we couldn't get in because the bishop had canceled the pilgrims' mass to ordain a dozen priests and deacons.

Samos, our next stop, was my last hope, a monastery that took pride in a centuries-long tradition of liturgy and scholarship. We would have to walk farther than any previous day to get there, but it would be worth it.

We had walked hard to make Samos before mass, and were resting in the *refugio* (once the monastery's stables) when a sharp-faced old monk burst in to announce the pilgrims-only tour of the cloisters. Anyone taking this tour must go to vespers. After that, the pilgrims' mass would be optional. In "twenty minutes exactly" he would open the locked gate beyond the *refugio*.

· · · · ·

Maria had gone to the pharmacy for blister supplies when the monk opened the gate and began shooing everyone in. I put one foot over the threshold and leaned out, looking for Maria. She just then rounded the corner. "Run!" I shouted. The monk looked out, saw Maria, and began closing the door just slowly enough to allow her to slip through. He made a loud show of slamming the door after her and locked it.

"Real frescoes," he muttered as he rushed us along an eighteenth-century cloister. Modern and not very good, I thought. One pilgrim asked what scenes these paintings depicted. The monk didn't acknowledge the questions. We raced after him across the garden, through a passage, into another cloister, up a stairway, along the upper cloister, and into a long, wood-paneled room furnished with pews and an altar. He herded us into the back pews and left. "That was the tour?" one pilgrim muttered. We waited silently.

Tall novices filed in by twos from a door near the altar. Tiny, frail old men in scapulars followed, the senior members of the community, our guide among them. They sang vespers well together and all filed out again. This pilgrims' mass will be good, I thought.

Our guide awaited us outside. He ordered a novice to herd out the twenty pilgrims who weren't going to mass. "Follow," he said to the rest of us. And off we went down a dark medieval stairway that the eighteenth-century renovators had overlooked. He slipped through a wrecked door of worn rough wood. We stepped after him into the vast brightness of the church we had seen from the hilltop. He was nowhere in sight. Ten of us took seats in a church big enough for a thousand.

I stared at the imposing rows of columns and arches, mathematically uniform down to the fluting. A few villagers filed through the main doors of the church and waited with us. I looked toward the high altar to say my prayers. Instead my attention fixed on twin statues flanking the altar, identical San Isidoros beheading identical Moors.

From somewhere past these sentinels, a tall old man in baggy street clothes led our guide to the altar. He was now vested for mass and carrying chalice and paten. The tall man placed the missal on the altar, but the priest set the cloth and vessels himself. He stood on tiptoes to reach the altar top, almost shoulder-height for him. He began reading the mass very fast, got frustrated when ribbon markers weren't where he wanted them, moved them, muttered, made his acolyte move the book, moved it back himself, and read on, pausing only briefly for a last glower at his acolyte. Readings, prayers and consecration flew hard and sharp as San Isidoro's sword.

His invitation to Communion sounded like a dare. His unveiled rage frustrated me and I felt ashamed for him, but lined up with the others for Communion anyway. This isn't it, I thought, walking forward. To my surprise, my eyes filled with tears as I received. **D**

Stay Where You Belong

WE WALKED A LONG DAY to Barbadelo, thirty kilometers in good warm weather. I was more in the mood to listen than talk so I asked Dad questions about religion, a topic I knew he couldn't resist. What biblical reason did the Vatican have not to ordain women? How did he decide to become ordained? How could he accept the Bible both as Word of God and a historical mess? We also talked about how, when I was four, he and Mom had made the decision to move from Idaho to San Francisco to help start Saint Gregory's.

We got into Barbadelo around three o'clock. The *refugio* was one of Galicia's handsome new *refugios*—white and green trimmed, all built from the same plans. It wasn't open yet. There were only a few other buildings nearby, all closed. We rested in the shade of an outdoor bandstand facing a dry field strewn with the trash and banner strings, leftovers from the local Saint James Fiesta.

Julio and Veronica arrived a few moments after us. "We planned a longer day, but my feet are *muy mal*," she told me. "But tell them how far we walked yesterday!" Julio said proudly. She laughed and shrugged her shoulders.

The *refugio* opened. We checked in together. The *hospitalera* led us upstairs. Twenty-two beds were split evenly between two identical dorm rooms. "Take your beds here," the *hospitalera* said, pointing to the shadier room. The adjoining bathroom's urinals told me that the architect had marked this room, "men's dorm." Seeing the other room, hot with afternoon sunlight, I felt grateful the *hospitalera* had us all share this room first.

Veronica was showering, and Julio, Dad and I were napping, when a pair of muscular cyclists barged in and threw their bags on two beds by the door. The *hospitalera* rushed in behind them. "*What* are you doing?"

"To sleep," the bigger one mumbled in broken Spanish. The argument began.

The *hospitalera* was furious that the cyclists had not found her to check them in, as any other pilgrim would have done. "I must save these beds first for pilgrims on foot!" She dragged them back downstairs, scolding them as she went. There were six empty beds in our room and twelve more in the other room, so I imagined she would let them stay. She just wants them to respect the rules, I thought to myself.

The cyclists returned and laid out their sleeping bags. They swore at her in German as they yanked gear from their bicycle packs. I watched them warily. Neither spoke to us.

My eyes were closed when shouts erupted from the bathroom.

"*Get out of here! Little bitch, just get out of here!*" the big cyclist was yelling.

"Use the stall!" A woman's voice. Veronica. I sat up and grabbed my stick.

"*It's a goddamned men's room! Look—urinals!*"

Dad and Julio leapt from their bunks at the far end of the room.

"This is *the* bathroom. *Refugios* do not have men's rooms."

"*Then watch me pee.*"

"*You* get out!" Veronica yelled. The man fled out the door, Veronica right behind him. She stood barefoot with wet hair, shaking her fist at him while holding her towel closed with her other hand. He spun around and pushed past Dad and Julio, marching out of the room like a general.

"Are you all right?" Julio asked.

"Yes," she said firmly, "quite all right."

"I will speak to him."

"No need," she said putting a hand on his arm. "I already have." *M*

Portomarín
· · · · ·

WE HEADED OUT FROM Barbadelo at about six, enjoying a cool, overcast morning. We passed an abandoned town, its ancient church locked and decaying, though the churchyard and graves were well maintained.

Around seven I looked longingly at a handmade sign leaning against a small house: *frambuesas*—raspberries! I imagined a small child selling tiny boxes of the delicate fruit to tired pilgrims. No one was up yet. We walked on.

I took the bar at the next hollow as our consolation. It was too early to rest, but the place was inviting and we didn't know when we would next find coffee. The family-owned bar was unfinished. Three generations of men continued building, while three generations of women served us.

As we started walking again, I felt a tiny pain on my left toe. My pilgrimage's second

· · · · ·

blister. We stopped and I took off my boot. "I'll get out the Betadyne," Dad said, putting down his bag. The blister was too small to puncture so we soaked a thread with the brown liquid, and pulled it through a needle. I pushed the needle into the blister and began dragging the thread through. Instantly I felt a precise stinging and pain shot up from my toe, through my back, to the hairs on my neck. I jumped up, shaking my hands and yelping. This was what Dad had been doing to himself? "It's pretty nasty stuff," Dad apologized. The pain cooled a little and I said, "I guess it's my sympathy blister."

By lunchtime the Camino emerged from the woods and we saw Portomarín on a hill across a reservoir. When the reservoir had been built some years back, the old riverside town's Romanesque church and its best buildings had been moved up to the hillside. We crossed a high concrete bridge into the town.

It had a good feel to it, a place where families spent the summers enjoying the hot weather. We found a grocery store and bought food for lunch and for breakfast the next morning. The day before Dad had dropped my camera, so we looked for a disposable camera to use during the rest of the trip. We found a small camera shop.

One of the great mysteries of Spanish commerce is how exactly products are paired together. In Córdoba I had lived near a makeup and house paint store. In Portomarín, the camera shop also sold shoes. "We might as well ask," I said to Dad.

"Yes, of course we have *plantillas*," the saleswoman replied, as she opened a drawer. "What is your size?"

She pulled out a pair of thick contoured insoles. Dad looked at them, pinching them between his fingers. We were both very quiet.

"I can get you another kind," she said turning toward the cut-to-fit insoles behind the counter. *"No!"* we both yelled.

"No, thank you," I said more calmly. Dad smiled, "*Son perfectos....*"

We paid the woman and left the store. Dad sat on a bench and took the old insoles out of his shoes and put the new pair in. He bounced on his feet. "These are great!"

Leaving Portomarín we crossed Torres creek by a steel footbridge. With every step our boots made great resounding booms. We played with the sound, banging our feet until the rhythmic sway of the bridge made us queasy. *M*

Best Day
· · · · · ·

DAD'S FEET began to heal with his new liners. On the uphill I struggled to keep up as he darted out in front of me and yelled, "Is that the best you can do?" I let go of mental calculations of distances and averages; with this new pace I knew we would make Santiago.

In Ventas de Narón we met a couple who had started walking in Barcelona. These were real walkers, their bodies subtly strong, their minds humble. Most days they walked forty kilometers, some days as far as sixty kilometers. After talking to them, we started our next day with a new determination.

We awoke at 5 a.m. before the alarm went off. Leaving the *refugio* I looked up at the clear night sky. Far from any city, the stars reminded us how the medieval pilgrims found their way through the night. The cool dawn lingered, and the path stayed level. The sun rose, but the fog quickly covered it.

We stopped in Palas de Rey after eleven kilometers to enjoy our mid-morning break. It was short. We had become addicted to walking, and sitting or standing still had us both antsy to go. As the day warmed up the sun seemed an indecisive prima donna, trying to convince us we wanted her to appear, then hiding from our lack of interest.

· · · · · ·

We passed a Celtic church with a carving so old the weather had eaten through the smooth stone until it looked like coral. I could only make out the pattern by standing at a distance. Predictably enough, Dad said, "I wish I could show your mother this."

Dad often talked of missing Mom. Every beautiful building was one he wanted to build for her; each vista was something that he wanted to share with her. When he smiled for no apparent reason, I knew he was thinking about her.

"Tell me about the first time you saw Mom," I said.

The story drifted to his first marriage, a union that produced my elder sister, Sasha. When I asked about that, Dad paused. "How much of this do you really want to know?"

As he spoke, he walked ahead of me—a person telling me stories of his young self, his depression, and the mistakes he saw in a failed marriage. Hearing this and thinking of my own failed love, I saw that our struggles were not so different.

We ended our day in silliness, singing our conversation to Beethoven's *Ode to Joy*, skipping down the hill toward the *refugio*, one of the most ancient of the Camino, waiting quietly by the banks of Rio Iso. At the bridge we saw pilgrims dangling their feet in the water and knew we'd join them in a moment. We arrived knowing we had just completed forty kilometers, our longest day on the whole Camino. *M*

THE CLOSER WE GOT to Santiago the more predictable the Camino became. On the road uniform concrete obelisks with the distance in kilometers to Santiago appeared regularly. No more yellow arrows. We saw several Galician *refugios* identical to Barbadelo. To get a certificate of completion a pilgrim needed to travel only sixty kilometers on foot, so many opted to walk only this last fraction of the pilgrimage. When we arrived in Arco O Pino, we were about four hours from Santiago. We decided not to go on so the next day would be short enough to arrive in time for the noon mass.

We were tired but pleased with our progress. We washed our clothes and found our bunks next to an American who was retracing his pilgrimage backward, returning on foot to Paris.

The *refugio* had a very large kitchen with multiple work stations. A group of twenty people was preparing a vegetarian feast and occupied most of the available space. I found a corner to work on our dinner and talked to a man from the group. They were from Madrid, followers of Gandhi who had walked the pilgrimage together in two-week segments each summer over four years. Their vegetarian feast (something almost unheard of in Spain) was to celebrate the last evening of their journey.

The man was about Dad's age. When he heard our blister saga and the treatment we used, he balked in horror. He took off his own shoe, a well-worn pair of sandal hand-me-downs from his son. He pointed to a fluid filled blister. "I won't even pop it. The body knows what to do. In time it will heal." I was skeptical of his medical logic, but jealous of his confidence.

Someone else in the crowd invited us to dinner, an invitation that got lost in language and cultural complications, so we just completed our efforts and ate outside. The group decorated the dining room with wildflowers and leaves, left, and then reappeared all dressed in

· · · · · ·

white for their feast. They began singing. I was tired and it was more energy than I could deal with. I told Dad I was going up to my bunk to sleep. Dad replied that he would meet me up there in a little bit.

The American was on his bunk, reading a paperback and tearing out pages as he finished them. "Less weight to carry in my pack," he said. Through the floor we could hear singing and laughing downstairs. "It seems a bit unfair," he said, "them taking over the whole common room."

"Well, I guess people are welcome to join them if they want to."

Dad returned in a flurry of excitement. "They are wonderful! Did you hear us singing? We exchanged addresses, and they promised to send me music." I felt left out and too tired to face all his exuberance. "I am going back down for their prayer meeting, Maria." He jumped up, and headed back downstairs. I rolled over and imagined writing a letter home,

> Dear Mom,
> Dad has thrown away all his black shirts and has run off with a group of
> Madrileño followers of Gandhi. He didn't say when, but he promised to return
> in white cotton clothing with good music for liturgy. *M*

AFTER THE LAST NIGHT'S PRAYERS with the Gandhi people and a good night's sleep, our last day began perfectly. We rose, packed silently, and slipped out the *refugio* door and into darkness, the first out that morning.

A single pair of headlights approached. We waited and watched the car pass by too slowly for the highway. The driver stared anxiously ahead, driving with stiff, artificial precision at parking-lot speed.

"Drunk driver coming home late," Maria theorized as we crossed the empty silence behind him and found a Camino marker pointing up into a tall, dense wood. Our penlights showed a new-graded gravel road. We turned our lights off. Silent blackness surrounded us except overhead, where the sky path paralleled the faintest ribbon of silver gray beneath our feet.

We didn't speak at all. I drank our silence like strong coffee, enjoying the complex rhythm of four feet and two sticks on the dimly luminous gravel. Our brisk pace felt very good. We walked side by side on the crown of the lane, pushing to make our appointment, the noon pilgrims' mass in the cathedral.

Too soon, we walked out of woods into sleeping suburban, streets, dark houses facing us level and square. Even though they slept, these commuters would be at work in Santiago before us.

Maria turned her flashlight on and found our smallish yellow arrow on the sidewalk pointing down a dead-end residential street. On the pavement just at the cul-de-sac, another arrow pointed into a vacant lot between two houses. I felt glad to be back in the woods.

The ground muffled our footsteps. Ghostly trees sloughed off gray for muted greens and browns, and dawning light showed the path's different sound matched a new surface, hard-

· · · · ·

packed reddish clay, new Camino; but we had it to ourselves. As we walked, the wooded path led uphill, the first sunlight touching the highest treetops with the brighter green of day.

Then the air shook—engine roar—then the grating of landing flaps engaging, and the sharp screech of doughnut tires hitting pavement. Seven o'clock. In quick succession two more planes touched down. We couldn't see them for the forest, though they sounded very close. "I wish people flying in to visit Saint James wouldn't crash into our silence so. My feet hurt."

I couldn't find a walking rhythm that would stop the pain of a new round of blisters. I was tired of hurting and even more tired of staying cheerful and optimistic. But we were so near, just ten kilometers, two hours' walk. I was angry with myself for saying my feet hurt, and angry with my blisters for spoiling our strong opening pace and preventing me from a heroic finish.

I wished Maria would express some appreciation for my suffering. Instead she tried to distract me with talking. My fault for speaking, I thought immediately. I didn't want to talk. All I wanted was an admiring pat on the back. She kept talking. Her chatter couldn't stop my blisters from hurting.

I chose to pay no attention and responded with hmmm's, agreeing grunts, and, whenever the melody of conversation and a pause seemed to call for it, the occasional "really?"

If I could just stay focused and suffer in peace, I thought, we'd be in Santiago soon. It had been a great pilgrimage. Unfortunately we weren't quite there yet and I wanted it to be over now. **D**

. . . . .

Failing

. . . . .

BEFORE WE REACHED SAMOS, I had completely forgotten that it was only a matter of time before we would arrive in Santiago. It never occurred to me that deciding to walk the forty kilometers from Ventas de Narón to Ribadiso would mean ending our pilgrimage a day sooner. In Arco O Pino I didn't think to make a sentimental event of our last night on the Camino. But that morning, just eighteen kilometers from the cathedral and with the pilgrims' mass starting at noon, there was no escaping it. This was our last day.

Eighteen kilometers didn't seem like much when we had set out, but after the first hour of walking it felt like too much. It was difficult to maintain a good steady pace on the hard concrete of suburban neighborhoods. I was tired and ready to be there, but knew our pilgrimage wasn't quite over yet.

The closer that we got to Santiago the more I could see my father's mood worsening. Another day I would have suggested a break, but with noon fast approaching there was no time. We raced against our own schedule.

I tried to relieve Dad's pain by giving him what I needed myself. I am a talker. I talk for pleasure, I talk to relieve pain. And so I began to talk, ranting on and on about any subject that popped into my head. I talked as if my mouth were attached to my feet, afraid that if I abandoned one, the other would quit. Dad wanted to suffer like a monk in silence and tried to tell me this. I didn't hear him over all my talking.

Topical subjects, things to do in Santiago, twentieth-century Spanish history, people I hated in college, only induced grunts and the occasional, "Can we not talk about this anymore?"

I tried witty banter, making a joke about being the milkman's child. "Maybe you should go walk with the milkman then," he replied.

"Maybe I wish I was walking with a not-so-grumpy father." Walking slightly ahead of me Dad mumbled, "Maybe I'm walking with the wrong daughter."

I stopped. Dad kept walking.

Sasha. He wants to walk with Sasha. Sasha, who thought me unprepared to do the Camino. Sasha, whose name I kept silently with me on the worst parts of the first day, promising myself, "I will prove her wrong." Sasha, my sister whose coming to live in our house ended my eight-year reign as eldest. Sasha, who shared a love of literature and reading with Dad while I could not. So this was the truth. All my attempts to become his adult daughter—and he already had one.

Anger saturated me, leaving nothing else, no words, no walking, nothing. This was *my* idea, *my* Spain, and *my* pilgrimage. He was just an invited guest. I looked at him, now stopped in the road some six feet ahead of me. Silently I promised myself, I would not cry.

"I can't believe you said that." *M*

King Lear
· · · · ·

"I have another daughter whose shape is kind and comfortable."
—*King Lear* Act 2, Scene 4

WE WERE ONLY a few hours from Santiago, but it felt like motion in place.

My feet kept hurting more, and the forest path kept turning oddly as we skirted the edge of the airport. Maria labored to draw me into the moment, but in my patient, suffering mode, I objected that I was grumpy and just wanted to be quiet. She tried to joke and tease

· · · · · ·

grumpiness to laughter. When I laughed it just made me angry, but still laughing, I told her I was very grumpy and really wanted to be quiet. She backed off from joking and offered sweet imaginings of arrival, a really hot shower, a nap, and days of leisure to heal my feet. I already held just these thoughts before me, the silent donkey's carrot. Hearing her speak them only annoyed me.

I insisted, vehemently, that if she could just let me sulk, I would find a way through.

She made more jokes and played affectionately with calling me "sulky." I felt pushed, and made, I told myself, a deflecting joke. I hoped she'd laugh and we could both walk into a little silence.

"Maybe I'm walking with the wrong daughter," I said.

It was a desperate tease to stop teasing.

She stopped walking, paused for a moment, and spoke almost in tears, "I can't believe you just said that to me. You invite yourself along on my pilgrimage, and then say such a thing on our last day!"

She had not taken it as a joke. I had hurt her. It wasn't supposed to end this way. All the daily caring for each other, our encouraging each other over weeks, had come to this wrong place: two people under stress, repeatedly misjudging what the other wanted or could take.

"I'm sorry. It was a joke. Let's keep walking," I said.

Stumbling and awkwardness belonged at the beginning. Our bodies and spirits were supposed to be tuned now by days of extended walking practice. By now, I thought, we should know how to walk and forgive our way through conflict. But here almost in sight of our destination, I'd thrown sharp teasing words that left us both wondering whether each of us knew the other.

In my journal entry, written only a few hours after this hard moment, I hear myself trying to cover this abyss:

· · · · · ·

Eighteen kilometers to Santiago. Poor Maria. I was exhausted and grumpy this morning. She is a good sport. Santiago itself is a delight … Maria kept nudging me awake through mass. When we stood, my legs were so tired that I had to lean on my arms or sit back down, but afterwards, it was Maria's turn to quit functioning. I found us a room in the nearest hostel. I am writing this after we've both showered and napped. We're feeling better.

What I wrote there skipped the harder truth of my stinging words in our last day. I was willing to write that we had walked three hundred miles and completed our pilgrimage exhausted. But our meandering shuffle following that darkly enchanted path? The forest that seemed to grow endlessly before us? The pointless twists and turns in the woods, while we could hear Santiago's airport and traffic near at hand? The very day's merciful ending eluding us for hours on end? And our fight, which still stung? I wrote refusing to acknowledge that we had traveled five hundred kilometers only to have a stupid, painful fight and feel lost and frustrated with each other. Our pilgrimage was supposed to end in elation at the Cathedral of St. James. We had accomplished so much together. How could we walk all that way and stumble into an aimless trek and a fight? When we did finally arrive, I wrote my journal entry to avoid the questions of just where we had got to. **D**

. . . . . .

PILGRIMS WE MET described feeling a little disappointed with Santiago. The city never seemed to meet up to their expectations. They felt lost and wanted to return to the "real" Camino, the way, the walking. We arrived realizing that we were not on a pilgrimage of destination and that Santiago itself could not surpass the three hundred miles before it.

By the time we stood in the old city I was lost in a haze. My body was sore and uncooperative as if angry with me. "We are here already! Why won't you let me lie down?"

It took some time to find the Cathedral for the pilgrims' noon mass. I don't remember much of the service, my mind numb with exhaustion. When the service called for us to stand, I leaned on the back of the pew in front of me to keep upright. Looking around, I saw Dad doing this too, and so many other dazed, exhausted, dirty pilgrims.

Just as I felt I might curl up on the Cathedral floor, the priest announced the arrival of the *Botafumeiro*, an incense-filled thurible, almost as tall as a person. It looked heavy and awkward as men in ceremonial gowns attached it to a rope as thick as an arm. The rope ran straight up to the dome of the Cathedral, into an elaborate system of pulleys and then back down to the floor. Once the rope and the *Botafumeiro* were properly in place, eight men began a first slow and calculated, and then kind of frantic, pulling on the rope that set the enormous censer swinging the entire breadth of the transept. The force of this pulling moved the censer in a parabolic suicide swing that had short moments of simply letting the *Botafumeiro* drop.

Through the holes that released the sweet-smelling smoke the incense was not just smoking, it was actually a small ball of fire. I watched its hypnotic swing, too impossibly tired to be as impressed as I should have been. The priest standing at the altar looked bored as the

Botafumeiro went flying past him, a mere two feet above the floor and some five feet in front of him.

After the service somehow Dad managed to find the Saint Philip Neri's seminary, a hotel in the summer. We both showered and I collapsed on my bed and awoke some hours later to the sound of Galician bagpipes coming from the square in front of the seminary.

Over the next three days the weather was cloudless and cool, unusually good, we were told. Every day we were there, bright sun on the Cathedral made the brown facade turn golden red. We drifted around town, structuring our days around meals, coffee, and an afternoon nap.

We took to shopping, looking happily at the heavy, awkward, and fragile gifts we now could afford to carry home, but bought the smaller ones that our walking had habituated us to. Dad bought Mom a pair of hand-made *azabache* (jet) earrings. I bought a small *azabache* pilgrim's shell necklace and began wearing it immediately.

Slowly we began to know the place a little. To recognize the doorman at the hotel and to joke with him. To settle on a restaurant we christened our own. To always order *pimientos de padron*, a local small green pepper seared in garlic and olive oil and sprinkled with sea salt.

As pilgrims we were part of the landscape. An Argentine film crew interviewed us about the Camino. I caught a middle-aged, overweight tourist in an elaborate costume, staff, and heavy brass shell around his neck, taking a picture of us.

We showed up to the noon mass each day to watch for pilgrim friends' arrivals. Luciano appeared at one of these, calling the Advil we gave him for his knee "the miracle pills."

Later that day we ran into a German couple we knew from the route. They complained that their flight wouldn't leave for another three days, and that they were stuck in the city.

. . . . . .

"There is nothing here!" said the man as he gestured down the street toward the Cathedral and seminary. I smiled sympathetically, understanding his sentiment and feeling glad I had not let my expectations trap me in the same blindness. *M*

Saying Goodbye
. . . . .

WE ARRIVED at the Madrid airport early in the morning. Separate flights would take us home. It was still quiet as we checked our luggage. With just our hats, walking sticks and my small bag we sat down side by side on the hard plastic seats that faced the security check. Just like the month before in the airport, our clothes caught the attention of other travelers. But this time I didn't feel self-conscious. I had nothing to prove.

My plane was leaving first. I watched the clock above airport security. The fluid, lazy movements of the second hand felt hypnotic. Dad turned to me and said, "You know, I think I have spent more uninterrupted time with you than I have spent with any other person on earth."

"Yeah," was all I could think to say. I looked up at the clock again. "Time to go." I gathered my things together, stood up, and began walking through security. I gave the officer my passport and ticket. I turned back to look at my Dad. He wasn't looking at me.

Buzzing florescent light and the off-white color of the walls unfairly aged him. He looked dazed, tired and ready to be home. I waited, wondering if he would look back and smile. He didn't. I put my stick on the x-ray machine and headed toward my gate. *M*

. . . . .

Now what?
· · · · · ·

SITTING ALONE on the plane ride home I was desperate to talk to someone about the Camino. I wanted to stand up and yell, "Something's happened to me!" The man next to me read his newspaper. The airline attendant stopped only long enough to refill my tomato juice. So I sat silently rubbing my *azabache* pilgrim shell necklace between my fingers.

Seven thousand miles from Santiago I immersed myself in the world of third grade, starting my first post-college job as an assistant teacher. Among the third graders my jet necklace was only "a shell for Miss Schell." I thought about the Camino constantly, but I held back talking about it, afraid of becoming tedious and boring.

"Yes, Maria, we know you walked the pilgrimage to Santiago,"

"Yes, Maria, we know you walked three hundred miles."

"Yes, Maria, we know it changed your life."

"Yes, Maria, we know it was a mystical, transformative … blah, blah, blah."

When I tried to explain the Camino, I felt stupid and trite. Words fell short and small. Within two months of my return I fell into a silent depression. The pilgrimage became my secret. Then Dad started this book. I left teaching to join him writing it. Completing it is another arrival, and beyond, I don't know yet. *M*

Walking Again

· · · · ·

FOURTEEN MONTHS LATER, Maria and I were deep into writing this book. I found satisfying and interesting thoughts and recollections of pilgrimage touching every task and pleasure of my life.

Like walking, writing is slow, and like our pilgrimage, this writing was an effort where Maria and I were sharing every step we took.

Then, unbelievably, I got word that both my parents were in a hospital in France. They had been traveling there for a couple of weeks when my mother had stabbing abdominal pains and a police-escorted ambulance race across the French countryside to the big hospital in Dijon. It was a life-threatening knot in her intestines. Mother's second emergency surgery there put my physician father in a second hospital with the same stabbing abdominal pains. When I learned the two of them were separated and helpless in a country where neither spoke the language, I dropped writing this to catch a plane with my brother and try to help them. It felt like abandoning Maria to walk our pilgrimage all by herself.

My brother and I arrived to find my dad on the mend. Dad's symptoms, the French doctors concluded, were sympathetic manifestations of his fear for his wife. Just knowing we were on our way had lessened his fear, and he felt readier to face what lay ahead with his sons beside him. For the next two weeks we three worked to encourage Mother's fight for her life. After three surgeries and a long time in an Intensive Care Unit where no one spoke English (Mother speaks no French), she was sinking into terrified hallucinations. We and the doctors feared she would die.

Daily walking in those weeks carried me back to the Camino. Each day my brother and I walked from our hotel through Dijon's old city and up the hill to the University Hospital complex to sit with Mother. On our way we talked cautiously about how Mom was doing,

· · · · ·

occasionally taking a diversion in the town. But my body whole-heartedly embraced the simple daily return to rhythmic lengthening and tensing of muscles from hip to knee, the calf-and-ankle push, the bend and push-off of the arched foot.

The walk to the hospital meant I could wait, and talk, and worry, and pray and share stories with my Dad. The walk back to the hotel meant I could sleep.

When I thought Mother would die, my mind went to our heavenly sense of arriving and rest in Santiago, and I held that for her. I stretched this hope to listen to Mother's fears and pray honestly, remembering mortality.

Anyone who has ever kept such vigil knows that at seventy-five the real question is, "When is she going to die?" But knowing mortality doesn't banish hope. I thought of medieval pilgrims who set out for Santiago because they were dying, but surprised family by returning home to Paris or Dijon with their stories of the Camino and of Santiago.

Mother didn't die. She flew home and survived a fourth surgery here and finally began to heal. Eight months later, we seem to have returned from this particular dying, but in Dijon I saw a little of how our pilgrimage continues. I remember arriving in Santiago and remember that good things don't end without grief, even when what comes at the end is good. After Santiago and Dijon our Camino continues, daily walking, daily discoveries of gratitude, daily surprises, not all of them joyful, and the reminder to keep on. **D**

. . . . . .